2. Invite members to pray short prayers. Tell them you will pray last. Lead in prayer after several have prayed. This period is not designed for a full-length prayer meeting.

Daily Quiet Time (10 minutes)

3. Share your personal plan for a daily quiet time. Do not mention the length of time unless someone asks you. You should emphasize the consistency more than the amount of time at this point. Note to members that they will learn more about the significance of their daily quiet times as they study the material in week 2 of their member books. Review the points in "How to Have a Quiet Time" on pages 19-20 of the member book.

Prayer Covenant List (10 minutes)

4. Call attention to "How to Use the Prayer-Covenant List" on page 43 in week 2.

5. Explain how to use the Prayer-Covenant List on the top of page 138 in the member book. Say, You have permission to photocopy the Prayer-Covenant List. You may want to make individual lists for various categories of prayer or for different days of the week. Ideally, you will have at least one list of requests for which you pray daily. Other requests may be prayed for on a weekly or a monthly schedule.

6. Say, List each request in specific terms so you will know when it is answered. For example, do not write, "Bless Aunt Dolly." Instead, ask that Aunt Dolly might be able to use her arm again. Record the date requested. If the Holy Spirit impress on you a particular Bible verse related to that request, write that verse in the appropriate column. (You may want to give a personal example.) Be alert to verses in your Bible reading that might apply to your request. Later, we will study more about the different ways God answers prayer. Leave two or three lines on which to write entries in the answer column. Your prayer may be answered in stages. Write the date when each prayer is answered.

7. Assure members that they are not expected to have enough prayer requests to fill all the lines. Suggest that they record only the requests that represent real concerns to them.

8. Tell members that they will be asked before session 2 to add at least five lost persons to their Prayer-Covenant Lists and to begin praying regularly for them.

9. Remind members that their prayer lists with dated answers may become the best evidence that they have to convince a skeptic of the concern and power of God.

10. Ask each person to share one request he or she has. Ask other members of the group to write that request on their Prayer-Covenant Lists.

Disciple's Cross Presentation (10/15 minutes)

11. Ask each member to pair with a member he or she has not yet worked with.

12. Instruct members to practice explaining and drawing for their partners the center of the Disciple's Cross and saying the verse that accompanies it. Both members will attempt to explain and draw the part of the cross they have learned. Remind them that they will add material each week to their presentation of the cross. By the end of this study they should be able to explain the Disciple's Cross in their own words.

Next Week's Assignments (5/10 minutes)

13. Ask members to look at "My Walk with the Master This Week" for week 2 on page 31 of the member book. Review the specific assignments. Make sure they understand how to complete each assignment.

14. Briefly preview the content of week 2. Ask members to complete week 2, "Live in the Word," before session 3. Tell them it will explain how they can grow closer to Christ as they learn to live in the Word by having a daily quiet time and memorizing Scripture.

15. Explain that they will be asked to get better acquainted with a member of the group during the next week. Remind them of the importance of this assignment so members can express support for each other.

Closure (5 minutes)

16. Announce the time and place for the next session.

17. Stand and join hands in a prayer of dismissal. Ask members to voice a one-sentence prayer. Ask volunteers to thank God for something that happened in today's session.

AFTER THE SESSION

❑ Evaluate the session by listing what you believe was effective. Consider ways to improve in future sessions.
❑ Make a Prayer-Covenant List for each person in your group so you can record needs to be prayed for and answers to your prayers. Pray daily for each person (see Phil. 1:6-8).
❑ Contact anyone who seems to need encouragement or counsel. Be a servant who helps group members grow.
❑ Invite two members to visit or minister with you during the week. Do not ask them to do anything they are not experienced in doing. The purpose is for them to observe. Before each visit, tell them what

you expect to find and do. After the visit, talk about why you conducted the visit as you did. Use the Roman Road gospel presentation (member book, pp. 103-7) or the Gospel in Hand presentation in *MasterLife 4: The Disciple's Mission* when you witness each week so that members can be familiar with it before they are asked to learn it. This is one of the most important skills to teach by example.

❑ Read "Before the Session" for Group Session 2 to evaluate the amount of preparation you will need. At the top of the first page of Group Session 2 material, record when you will prepare.

❑ Carefully study week 3 and do all the exercises in the member book. You will preview week 3 for members during session 2.

Split-Session Plan

FIRST WEEK

Follow part 1 of session 1 as it is outlined in the Standard Plan except for the following adjustments.

1. Instead of asking group members to share about the inventory, which they will take during the second week of the Split-Session Plan, ask for volunteers to share how they felt when they were asked about what priority Christ had in their lives. Do not ask for specific confessions; but if any members would like to share their feelings, allow time for them to do so. Emphasize that, as a group, you will help each other grow in challenging areas.

2. Lead "Spend Time with the Master," by reviewing items 4-10. Items 11-13 pertain to material members will study next week.

3. Call attention to the fact that your group is using the Split-Session Plan. This means that members will check off only the assignments that pertain to the material they have studied that week. For example, members were assigned only days 1-3 for the first week of this session. Therefore, they would not be able to check off the assignment about studying the World-Awareness Map because that assignment does not appear until day 4. The other assignments will be done the following week. During the preview time, preview only the assignments they will be responsible for next week.

SECOND WEEK

Follow the Standard Plan for part 2 of session 1 with the following changes. Use shorter times for each activity to allow for these activities.

1. Adjust the opening group time as suggested in part 2 to begin with the inventory discussion since members took the inventory as part of

their second week's work. Then continue with activities listed under Group Time.

2. Pair members with persons other than their spouses. Each member of the pair should check the other person's "My Walk with the Master This Week." The boxes with the vertical marks should be verified and marked with horizontal lines. Luke 9:23 should be quoted accurately by each member before that assignment is marked.

3. Spend about three minutes reviewing what members learned the first week in "Spend Time with the Master." Ask volunteers to summarize important points from last week. Then move on to questions 11-13.

4. Preview next week's assignments. Assign members days 1-3 in week 2, "Live in the Word." Members are to complete only assignments that pertain to the material they study this week.

One-to-One Study Plan

This session can be done by following the Standard Plan. Adapt the One-to-One Study Plan to the needs of the individual as you go. Future sessions will require more modification because of additional group activities. You may include the following options.

1. If you have extra time this week, give the person an opportunity to ask questions or to explore other areas he or she is interested in.

2. When discussing the inventory, go into more detail by asking the person to answer the questions at the conclusion of the inventory. Offer any help needed.

GROUP SESSION 2

Live in the Word

Session Goals
By the end of this session, members will be able to demonstrate their progress toward *MasterLife* goals by ...
- giving and receiving support from group members on problems they may be having with weekly assignments;
- completing assignments for week 2;
- explaining the lower bar of the *Disciple's Cross;*
- making Prayer-Covenant Lists and praying for the requests of group members.

Standard Plan

BEFORE THE SESSION

❑ Review week 2 and read and complete the learning activities for week 3 of *MasterLife 1: The Disciple's Cross* to stay ahead of the group.

❑ Call group members and ask how they are doing with their assignments; encourage them in their work.

❑ Pray daily for each member of the group. Ask the Lord to give you wisdom to prepare for and lead the group session.

❑ Master this week's material in the leader guide.

❑ Review the goals for this session.

❑ Check with the host or hostess to be sure he or she is ready for the group this week.

❑ Arrange the meeting place so that members can sit in a circle.

❑ Have pens or pencils and extra blank paper on hand for the session.

DURING THE SESSION

PART 1 (45/60 minutes)

Introduction (25/30 minutes)

1. Begin the session on time even if all members are not present. The objective of this period is to allow members to share their progress and any problems they are having with *MasterLife*. Begin with prayer.

2. Ask several persons to share one good experience related to completing their assignments this week. Limit this sharing to five minutes.

3. Take five minutes for members to identify any problems they may be having with any of the assignments. Ask other group members to suggest ways to solve these problems.

4. Ask members for reports on how they are doing with keeping a Prayer-Covenant List. Ask each person to volunteer one request that he or she put on the list during the week. Invite members to pray a sentence prayer for the request the person on his or her right mentioned.

5. Instruct group members to pair up and quote John 8:31-32 to each other. Make sure that husbands and wives are not paired together. While members work in pairs, they can check each other's "My Walk with the Master This Week" and draw the horizontal line in the member's diamond boxes after verifying completed work. Encourage the pairs to share their strong and weak points in completing the assignments.

"Live in the Word" (20/30 minutes)
Choose from the following items appropriate questions and activities for your group's study. Do not exceed the time allowance.

6. Ask, Which of the four reasons given for having a quiet time is the most important to you? Why? (The first listing of these four reasons is on p. 35 of the member book.) Ask them to suggest other reasons a quiet time is important.

7. Ask members to share benefits they see in a quiet time. Ask members to write the benefits in the margins of their workbooks as group members mention them.

8. Call for volunteers to tell how important a special time with God seemed to each of the following biblical characters: David, Daniel, John the Baptist, Jesus.

9. Ask, How do you know a special time with God was important to the person just mentioned? Say, The reasons you gave are observable ways we can evaluate how important a personal time with God is to us.

10. Ask members to write in the margins of their member books these items: eating, fellowship with family, personal cleanliness, work, personal time with God. Ask them to rank them 1 (highest priority) through 5 (lowest priority). Then, ask, What did you learn about yourself?

11. Tell your experience of establishing a quiet time.

12. Ask a volunteer to share a time God helped him or her make a decision after seeking answers from His Word in a quiet time.

13. Ask a volunteer to tell what he or she would need to give up in order to establish a regular time of fellowship with God.

14. Remind group members that before next week they will be asked to share with a friend their testimony of having a quiet time with someone who needs to develop this practice.

15. Ask members to pray with you. Voice a prayer asking God to help group members make a daily quiet time a part of their lives.

Take a stand-up break. Invite participants to help themselves to refreshments.

PART 2 (45/60 minutes)

Prayer Time (10/15 minutes)
1. Ask members to mention specific praises they have regarding their experiences in *MasterLife* so far.

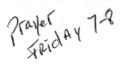

Prayer
Friday 7-8

2. Suggest that each member pray a short prayer of thanksgiving for the praise he or she just mentioned. Pray a brief prayer and invite volunteers to pray also.

The Disciple's Cross (25 minutes)

3. Form two small groups to practice presenting the Disciple's Cross. Two members of each small group will present the center circle of the Disciple's Cross. Two other members will present the lower bar of the Disciple's Cross. Other members of the group, if any, can indicate what points members did not cover in the presentation. Explain, The purpose of this activity is to make sure each person has gained an understanding of the elements in the Disciple's Cross learned so far. Each of you is responsible for learning the presentation in your own words and having that presentation affirmed by another member of our group. You may move at your own pace, but each of you should master the complete Disciple's Cross presentation by the end of week 6.

Next Week's Assignments (15 minutes)

4. Ask members to look at "My Walk with the Master This Week" for week 3 on page 53 of the member book. Review the specific assignments. Make sure the members understand how to complete each one.

5. Preview the content of week 3 briefly. Ask members to complete week 3, "Pray in Faith," before session 3. Tell them it will explain how they can grow in their relationship with Christ through praying in faith.

6. Call attention to the assignment about showing God's love to a person who is not a Christian. Explain that members may decide for themselves how to show love to this person. Share any experiences you have in relating in this way to a person who is not a Christian.

7. Talk about opportunities to get together with members or take them with you as you witness or minister. Times together outside the regular meeting period can be the best for helping people grow as disciples.

Closure (5 minutes)

8. Announce the time and place for the next meeting.

9. Stand and join hands. Invite members to voice a one-sentence prayer for the person on his or her right. Say, Ask God to help this member grow in his or her relationship with God through _MasterLife_.

AFTER THE SESSION

❑ Use the following questions to evaluate how well you led the session.
- Did everyone participate in the discussions?
- Did I affirm members for what they did well?

> • Did I encourage those who are having a difficult time?
> • Did members understand my explanations?

❑ Talk individually with members who are not keeping up with the group.
> • If they lack motivation, discuss reasons for their feelings.
> • If they lack time, help them determine how to use time wisely.
> • If they lack consistency, help them with self-discipline by showing them how to plan. Help them find a partner in the group who will check with them periodically.
> • If they lack understanding, clarify the "how to" by doing the activity with them.

❑ Take a couple of members with you as you minister or witness.

❑ Ask one member to be your assistant. The person may be your spouse. This person will assist in leading sessions and other group activities during the weeks ahead. Spend adequate time training this person to help you lead the group. This leader guide will give suggestions for involving this person in assisting you.

❑ Read "Before the Session" for Group Session 3. Evaluate the amount of preparation you will need for the next group session. At the top of the first page of session 3, record when you will prepare.

❑ Carefully study week 4 and do all the exercises in the member book. You will preview week 4 for members during session 4.

Split-Session Plan

FIRST WEEK
Follow part 1 of the session as it is outlined in the Standard Plan except for the following adjustments.

1. When you lead the session "Live in the Word," review items 6-10 only. You will review the remaining items next week.

2. Remind members that they will check off only those assignments that pertain to the material they have studied that week. For example, members were assigned only days 1-3 for the first week of this session. Therefore, they would not be able to check off the assignment about adding lost persons to their Prayer-Covenant Lists because that assignment does not appear until day 4. The other assignments will be done the following week. Preview only the assignments they will be responsible for next week.

SECOND WEEK
Follow the Standard Plan, part 2. Use shorter times for each activity to allow for the following additional activities.

1. Pair members with persons other than their spouses. Each member of the pair should check the other person's "My Walk with the Master This Week." The boxes with the vertical marks should be verified and crossed off. John 8:31-32 should be quoted accurately by each member before that assignment is marked off.

2. Lead the study "Live in the Word." Spend about three minutes reviewing what members learned during the first week. Ask volunteers to summarize important points from last week's study. Then move on to items 11-14.

3. Preview next week's assignments. Assign members days 1-3 in week 3, "Pray in Faith." Members are to complete only assignments that pertain to the material they study the first week.

One-to-One Study Plan

Follow the instructions in the Standard Plan with the exception of asking the individual to respond to all questions. When discussing the quiet time, go into detail by asking the person to discuss particulars of his or her efforts at having a quiet time. Be prepared to share your experiences as well.

GROUP SESSION 3

Pray in Faith

Session Goals

By the end of this session, members will be able to demonstrate their progress in achieving the *MasterLife* goals by ...
- incorporating thanksgiving, praise, confession, and asking into their prayer time;
- completing week 3 assignments;
- explaining the upper bar of the Disciple's Cross;
- telling group members how they showed love to non-Christians;
- praying for their personal needs and the needs of others.

Standard Plan

BEFORE THE SESSION
❑ Review week 3 and read and complete the learning activities for week 4 of *MasterLife 1: The Disciple's Cross* to stay ahead of the group.

❏ Pray daily for each member of your group.

❏ Master this week's material in the leader guide.

❏ Review the goals for this session.

❏ Check with the host or hostess to be sure he or she is ready for the group this week.

❏ Arrange the meeting place so that members can sit in a circle.

❏ Have pens or pencils and extra blank paper on hand for the session.

❏ Use the MasterTime form on page 138 in the member book to schedule your time and determine your priorities. Be able to share from your experience how this has helped you. Consider reading other material on time management.

Remember that allowing members to share freely is far more important than sticking legalistically to a plan you develop for the group session. Group members sometimes arrive at a session eager to tell about something that happened in their lives during the week related to that week's content. Be sensitive to this need, and be flexible. Allow God to work in your group. Provide opportunities for everyone to respond during the session.

DURING THE SESSION

PART 1 (45/60 minutes)

Introduction (25/30 minutes)

1. Arrive early and fellowship with members as they arrive. Be alert and available to discuss any questions they may have. Begin on time.

2. Ask volunteers to share needs in their lives. Begin by sharing one of your own needs. If you are open and honest, it will set the stage and make it easier for others to share their needs.

3. Ask if anyone has an update on any prayer requests that group members have mentioned.

4. Lead the group to pray short prayers related to personal needs or the prayer requests mentioned.

5. Pair members with persons other than their spouses. Ask members to check each other's "My Walk with the Master This Week." Members can use any extra time to review memory verses.

"Pray in Faith" (25/30 minutes)

Choose from the following list appropriate questions and activities for your group's study. Do not exceed the time allowance.

6. Invite a volunteer to share about an experience of praying on the basis of what he or she wanted rather than seeking God's will first (member book, p. 55). Tell your own experience in this area.

7. Call for volunteers to tell which of their Prayer-Covenant List requests they have seen answered.

8. Ask members why they believe thanksgiving and praising God occur first in prayer. Invite volunteers to share benefits they have experienced from coming before the Father with praise and thanksgiving first.

9. Ask, Which name of God explained in day 3 has been most helpful to you in learning to praise Him? Allow several members to respond.

10. Ask, How do we distinguish between praising God and thanking Him?

11. Ask, Why do you believe confessing sin is important? Invite a volunteer to share how he or she found that confessing sin helped restore a right relationship with God.

12. Invite a volunteer to tell about a time when he or she prayed with the wrong motivation or for an outcome that he or she later saw would not be Christ-honoring.

13. Invite several members to share one of the personal needs they listed in the member book on pages 69-70. Voice a prayer asking God to help group members with the specific requests mentioned.

14. Discuss why group members believe God wants them to intercede for others. Ask each group member to pray silently for someone on his or her Prayer-Covenant List.

15. Ask two or three volunteers to answer these questions: Which of the four types of prayers is the easiest for you to pray? Which is most challenging? Why?

Take a stand-up break. Invite participants to help themselves to refreshments.

PART 2 (45/60 minutes)

Call to Prayer (5/10 minutes)
1. Invite the group to come back together. Ask members to describe their experiences this past week in showing God's love to a person who is not a Christian. Ask group members to voice prayers for concerns others have mentioned regarding these non-Christian friends.

The Disciple's Cross (15/20 minutes)

2. Ask each member to pair with a person with whom he or she has not yet worked. Instruct each person to present to the other in his or her own words the material learned so far on the Disciple's Cross. Members have likely mastered the vertical bar and the center circle. Remind them that they may move at their own pace, but everyone is expected to master the complete Disciple's Cross presentation by the end of week 6.

MasterTime (15/20 minutes)

3. Say, Many members may find it difficult to add the *MasterLife* assignments to an already busy life. This training will help you learn to manage your time better and rethink your priorities. Setting goals and making long-range plans will enable you to do the most important tasks first.

4. Briefly introduce "Redeeming the Time" on page 84 in the member book by summarizing the key thoughts.

5. Introduce the MasterTime form on page 138 in the member book as a vehicle to help members set priorities and manage their time. Say, To manage time is to manage life.

6. Ask members to take notes as you explain how to use time wisely. You may refer to "How to Use MasterTime" (member book, pp. 88-89). Members will study the material later, but they should take notes now to help them learn. Explain each point, including the following:
- *Trust the Lord*. Begin by listing the activities you will do as a part of walking with the Master for this time period.
- *Plan your daily work*. Explain that members should use a few minutes at the beginning or end of the day to plan their use of time for the next 24 hours.
- *Ask the Lord*. Encourage members to pray as they make their plans.
- *Depend on the Lord*. Give examples of how you deal with interruptions.
- *Discipline yourself*. Encourage members to master their time but not to become a slave of their planning. We are not trying to reduce spontaneity but to encourage the wise use of time.
- *Leave the results to God*. Tell members to work when they should but to leave for tomorrow tasks they cannot finish. Worrying or becoming a workaholic interferes with the best use of time.

Next Week's Assignments (5 minutes)

7. Ask members to look at "My Walk with the Master This Week" for week 4 (member book, p. 73) and preview the specific assignments. Make sure the members understand how to complete each assignment.

8. Briefly preview the content of week 4. Ask members to complete week 4, "Fellowship with Believers," before session 4. Tell them the material will explain how they can grow in their relationship with Christ through fellowship with believers.

9. Call attention to the assignment about befriending someone in the church who is not a close friend or is not in the *MasterLife* group. Tell members they are to decide the best way to befriend the persons they choose.

Closure (5 minutes)

10. Offer individual help outside class if needed. Some members may feel overwhelmed by the amount of work or may feel stuck on an aspect of their work, such as Scripture memorization. Encourage members to contact you if they need help.

11. Answer any questions members may have. Close with prayer.

AFTER THE SESSION

❑ Use the following questions to evaluate how well you led the session.
  • Do members care for each other? Are they trusting each other? Are they becoming more open with each other?
  • Are there blocks in communication?
  • Are spouses relating well as group members?
  • Are members responding well to my leadership?
  • Is the group becoming cliquish? Do I need to encourage members to keep reaching out?
  • Do some members show undesirable attitudes toward other members? Should I take them visiting together and/or pair them up more often?
  • Are members helping disciple each other?
  • Do they see me as a growing disciple who also is learning from them?

❑ Continue to invite members to go witnessing and ministering with you. Take them on church visitation or hospital calls.

❑ Call or see all members of the group this week to encourage, enable, or challenge them as needed. Some will be struggling over how to manage time so they can complete their assignments. Remember that you are their servant. Involve your assistant in helping you.

❑ Read "Before the Session" for Group Session 4 to evaluate the amount of time you will need to prepare for the next group session. Record at the top of the first page of the Group Session 4 material when you will prepare.

❑ Carefully study week 5 and do all the exercises in the member book. You will preview week 5 for members during session 4.

Split-Session Plan

FIRST WEEK
Follow part 1 of the session as it is outlined except for the following adjustments. Use shorter times so you can accomplish all the activities.

1. Lead "Spend Time with the Master." Review items 6-10 only. The remaining items pertain to material members will study next week.

2. As you close this first week, ask members to describe their experiences this past week in showing God's love to a person who is not a Christian. Ask group members to voice prayers for concerns others have mentioned regarding these non-Christian friends.

3. Preview next week's assignments. Assign members days 4-5 in the study. Remind them to check off only those assignments that pertain to the material they have studied that week.

SECOND WEEK
Follow the Standard Plan, part 2, with the following alterations. Shorten times for each activity to allow for the following.

1. Begin with prayer. Instead of the prayer time for non-Christian friends, which members did in last week's session, ask them to share with someone other than their spouse about particular challenges they are facing as they study *MasterLife*. As the leader, voice the prayer, mentioning the needs members have shared.

2. Pair each member with someone other than his or her spouse. Each member of the pair should check the other person's "My Walk with the Master This Week." The boxes with the vertical marks should be verified and crossed off. John 15:7 should be quoted accurately by each member before that assignment is marked off.

One-to-One Plan

Follow instructions for the Standard Plan, with the following suggested variation. Give adequate time to help the person incorporate praying in faith into his or her life.

1. Help the person plan the next day's activities, using the MasterTime form.

2. If the person is having difficulty understanding where he or she wastes time, ask the person to keep a log of what he or she does for each

15-minute segment of time during the following week. This will be a time-consuming activity for the week, but it will reveal where time is being wasted and help the person plan to control it better in the future.

GROUP SESSION 4

Fellowship with Believers

Session Goals

By the end of this session, members will be able to demonstrate their progress in achieving the *MasterLife* goals by …
- sharing about their progress in having a quiet time;
- completing assignments for week 4;
- explaining the right crossbar of the Disciple's Cross;
- managing their time efficiently for the following week;
- sharing about their experiences in befriending someone who is not in their immediate circle of friends.

Standard Plan

BEFORE THE SESSION
❏ Review this week's material and complete the learning activities for week 5 of *MasterLife 1: The Disciple's Cross* so you can stay ahead of the group.
❏ Pray daily for each member of your group.
❏ Master this week's material in the leader guide.
❏ Review the goals for this session.
❏ Check with the host or hostess to be sure he or she is ready for the group this week.
❏ Arrange the meeting place so that members can sit in a circle.
❏ Have pens or pencils and extra blank paper on hand for the session.
❏ Begin making plans for the Growing Disciples Workshop. Prepare to brief members on the plans at the close of this session. Make the following arrangements.
  - *Meeting place.* Select a meeting site at the church or choose another adequate setting.
  - *Time.* Three hours are recommended; 2½ hours are the minimum. The workshop could be scheduled on a Saturday morning or Saturday afternoon, on a weeknight with an early meal preceding it, on a Sunday afternoon after a covered-dish meal, or on two weeknights. Select the time most workable to group members.
  - *Food/refreshments.* Refreshments should be prepared for break.

You might suggest that members bring favorite snacks for break time. If a meal is involved, suggestions include a meal served by the church, a covered-dish dinner, or a light lunch if you are meeting on Saturday or Sunday.

- *Supplies.* Newsprint/butcher paper or a large chalkboard for drawing; extra pens or pencils and paper. Have on hand copies of *MasterLife 2: The Disciple's Personality* for those who commit to continuing their *MasterLife* study.
- *Cost.* You may want to charge a fee to cover meals/snacks if members do not provide these. Also alert members that they will want to come prepared to pay for *MasterLife 2: The Disciple's Personality.*

❑ Prepare a copy of each of the following case studies for the Scripture-memory activity.

Case Study 1: Imagine that you are part of a group of Christians who have been put in jail. Your Bible has been taken from you. You want to reproduce the Bible word-perfect. How would you pool your knowledge to help each other memorize the Bible so you could remember the Word if you were later sent to separate cells?

Case Study 2: You are part of a group of teachers who work with students with learning disabilities. The students have average intelligence but find it difficult to read and remember. Nevertheless, they are eager to learn. What would you do to help them memorize Scripture?

Case Study 3: You are one of a group of teachers who work with underprivileged teenagers. These teenagers ride the church bus. They see no need for Scripture memorization. What could you do to convince them of the importance of Scripture memorization?

Case Study 4: You have moved to another city and joined a church. You have been asked to lead Scripture-memorization sessions for a group of adults in discipleship training. The members of the group give the usual excuses, such as:
- "I can't memorize."
- "I forget it as soon as I memorize it."
- "I've gotten along all right so far without Scripture memorization."
- "I don't have time."

What could you tell this group to help them make Scripture memorization a lifestyle?

❑ Review "How to Use MasterTime" on page 88 in the member book, and be prepared to answer any questions.
❑ Take a different person or persons visiting or ministering with you.

DURING THE SESSION

PART 1 (45/60 minutes)

Introduction (20/25 minutes)
1. Ask how many benefited from using MasterTime this week. Ask members to share ways they have been helped.

2. Ask members to share their problems with time management.

3. Give suggestions based on "How to Use MasterTime" (member book, p. 88) and "Redeeming the Time" (member book, p. 84). Encourage members to use time wisely by planning and letting the Master guide them.

4. Ask members to report how many times they had a quiet time during the week. Let each member share openly. Highlight that a place to mark each day was provided in "My Walk with the Master This Week" (member book, p. 73).

5. Praise God for progress members have made to this point. By now they should be able to have a quiet time at least five days of seven.

6. Ask members to share ways they have learned to overcome problems connected with setting aside a quiet time. Encourage them to support and help each other.

7. Pair members with persons other than their spouses to check each other's "My Walk with the Master This Week."

"Fellowship with Believers" (25/35 minutes)
Choose from the following list appropriate questions and activities for your group's study. Do not exceed the time allowance.

8. Ask a volunteer to share about an experience of trying to go it alone as a Christian rather than staying connected to the fellowship of believers (see member book, p. 77). Share your experience in this area.

9. Ask, Why is someone who professes to be a Christian, yet does not attend church, living outside God's will? *(Christ commands us to love each other and to encourage each other in the body of Christ. To do otherwise is disregarding God's Word.)*

10. Ask, Would someone tell about a time when he or she found it especially meaningful to fellowship with Christians? Allow two or three members to respond.

11. Ask volunteers to share their answers to the case studies of Anita and Charles on page 78 of the member book. Ask, Have any of you had an experience with befriending someone in need as these two case stories illustrate? Encourage members to share circumstances, not names.

12. Invite members to tell how they would answer a fellow believer who says, "I can worship God far better when I'm enjoying nature at leisure than I can in a church on Sunday morning." Ask members to share situations in their lives in which they struggled with issues about regular participation in the body of Christ.

13. Ask members to respond to the statement in the exercise on page 82 of the member book: "Friends care enough to confront one another in love if necessary." Ask, Do you believe that Christians can confront each other in a loving, Christ-honoring way? Would someone share about a time when they confronted another person this way?

14. Ask, What was the difference between the relationship of a servant and his master and the relationship the disciples had with Jesus? (See p. 86, member book.) (*A servant would not know His Master's business. Jesus called the disciples friends.*)

15. Ask, What were the three reasons Jesus gave for choosing His disciples? (see p. 86, member book). (*To bear fruit, to ask the Father in His name, and to love one another.*)

16. Ask several volunteers to share about a time when they were witnessing and their fellowship with other believers supported them.

17. Invite each group member to pray silently that he or she will continue to see the difference that fellowship with other believers can make in living life in Christ.

Take a stand-up break. Invite participants to help themselves to refreshments.

PART 2 (45/60 minutes)

Prayer Time (15 minutes)
1. Call the group together. Ask members to describe briefly their experiences this past week in befriending someone who is not in their close circle of friends or in the *MasterLife* group. Emphasize that members do

not need to give the names of the persons they befriended but merely describe circumstances. Ask group members to voice prayers for concerns others have mentioned regarding these situations.

The Disciple's Cross (5/10 minutes)
2. Ask each member to pair with a person with whom he or she has not yet worked. Instruct each person to present to the other in his or her own words the material learned so far on the Disciple's Cross. Members should have mastered the center circle, the vertical bar, and the right crossbar. Remind members that they will be able to explain the complete Disciple's Cross in their own words by the end of week 6.

Next Week's Assignments (20/30 minutes)
3. Focus the group's attention on "How to Memorize Scripture" (member book, p. 112). Ask members to remain in pairs. Have each pair discuss one of the case studies you prepared. Ask them to compile a one-minute report for the group. If you have more than four pairs, let extra people join a pair for this discussion.

4. Ask each pair to report on their case study and tell in about one minute how they would attempt to solve the problem. Ask members to take notes on helpful ideas they can use for Scripture memorization. After the reports ask each member to tell one idea he or she noted.

5. Ask members to turn to "Reasons to Memorize Scripture" on page 110 in the member book. Review the reasons for Scripture memorization and illustrate them from your personal experiences. Encourage members to read Bible references related to the reasons during the next week. Emphasize each practical suggestion that "How to Memorize Scripture" gives.

6. Preview other assignments for next week. Ask members to look at "My Walk with the Master This Week" for week 5 on page 91 and preview the specific assignments. Make sure the members understand how to complete each assignment.

7. Preview the content of week 5 briefly. Ask members to complete week 5, "Witness to the World," before Group Session 5. Tell them it will help them bear witness to Christ and to their relationship with Him.

8. Announce plans for the Growing Disciples Workshop. Announce the time, date, and place. Discuss plans for food and snacks. Answer questions members might have. Make sure everyone understands that this workshop is not an optional activity but is a time to bring completion and experience celebration for all that members have accomplished. All assignments are to be completed before the workshop.

Closure (5 minutes)

9. Ask members to review "My Walk with the Master This Week" at the beginning of each week's study they have completed so far. Suggest that they have each item checked off as soon as possible to keep these activities from accumulating at the end of the book. Remind them that everyone needs to complete all items before the group moves on to *MasterLife 2: The Disciple's Personality.*

10. Announce next week's meeting place and time. Close with prayer.

AFTER THE SESSION

❑ Contact persons who are having difficulty completing their assignments. Ask if you can do anything to help.

❑ Take two members with you to minister or to witness. Members will find it easier to minister or witness if they have been with someone else under these circumstances. As you witness, try to use the Roman Road gospel presentation described in week 5.

❑ Pray daily for all members. Remember their prayer requests. Pray that they will be successful in hiding God's Word in their hearts.

❑ Continue to work on arrangements for the Growing Disciples Workshop, especially if you have decided to have the workshop away from your regular meeting site.

❑ Read "Before the Session" for Group Session 5 to evaluate the amount of time you will need to prepare for the next group session. At the beginning of session 5 material, record when you will prepare.

❑ Carefully study week 6 and do all the exercises in the member book. You will preview week 6 for members during session 5.

Split-Session Plan

FIRST WEEK

Follow part 1 of the session as it is outlined except for the following adjustments.

1. Instead of asking group members to share about their use of MasterTime (which they will begin using during the second week of this session), ask for volunteers to tell about their experiences in sharing with someone how they have grown in Christ from the practice of memorizing Scripture. Call the group to prayer. As leader, thank God for the members' experiences in memorizing Scripture. Ask God to help them grow in their abilities to commit Scripture to memory.

2. Lead the study "Fellowship with Believers." Review items 8-12 only. The remaining items pertain to material for next week.

3. Preview next week's assignments. Assign members days 4-5 in the study. Remind them to check off only those assignments that pertain to the material they have studied that week. The other assignments will be done the following week.

SECOND WEEK

Follow the Standard Plan, part 2, with the following alterations. Use shorter times for each activity to allow for the adaptations.

1. Ask members to share about their use of MasterTime since members began to use MasterTime as part of their second week's work for the study "Fellowship with Believers." Use the shorter times suggested in order to accommodate this discussion.

2. Pair members with persons other than their spouses. Each member of the pair should check the other person's "My Walk with the Master This Week." The boxes with the vertical marks should be verified and crossed off. John 13:34-35 should be quoted accurately by each member before that assignment is marked off.

3. Lead the study "Fellowship with Believers." Spend about three minutes reviewing what members learned during the first week in this study. Ask for volunteers to summarize important points from last week's study. Then move on to items 13-17 in part 1.

4. Preview next week's assignments. Assign members days 1-3 in the study "Witness to the World." Members are to complete only assignments that pertain to the material they study this week. (5 minutes)

One-to-One Plan

Follow instructions in the Standard Plan. Select any of the following adjustments to make your one-to-one experience more effective.

1. Check your partner's time log. If you asked the person to make a time log, analyze it. Look for the following.
   - Wasted time.
   - Interruptions not dealt with appropriately.
   - Lack of organization in doing tasks of a similar nature.
   - Tasks that could have been delegated to others.
   - Not gathering necessary materials before starting a task.
   - Insufficient planning.
   - How time totals for tasks compared with stated priorities.
   - How to plan and utilize time better.

2. Review your partner's notes on the Daily Master Communication Guides for the week. If the person is having difficulty having a consistent quiet time, you may suggest calling each morning this week when you have your quiet time.

3. During the study, be frank about any battle you may have had in failing to draw spiritual nourishment from the fellowship of believers. Share suggestions you have found helpful in benefiting from your fellowship with God's people.

4. Present the material related to the left crossbar of the Disciple's Cross, and ask your partner to note anything different from the presentation in *MasterLife*.

GROUP SESSION 5

Witness to the World

> **Session Goals**
> By the end of this session, members will be able to demonstrate their progress toward *MasterLife* goals by ...
> • reporting on a new friend who is a non-Christian and praying for the non-Christian friends of others;
> • completing assignments for week 5;
> • explaining the left crossbar of the Disciple's Cross;
> • giving and receiving support on problems that arise with Scripture memorization.

Standard Plan

BEFORE THE SESSION
❏ Review week 5 and read and complete the learning activities for week 6 of *MasterLife 1: The Disciple's Cross* to stay ahead of the group.
❏ Pray daily for each member of your group.
❏ Master this week's material in the leader guide.
❏ Review the goals for this session.
❏ Check with the host or hostess to be sure he or she is ready for the group this week.
❏ Arrange the meeting place so that members can sit in a circle.
❏ Have pens or pencils and extra blank paper on hand for the session.
❏ Review "How to Memorize Scripture" (member book, p. 112).
❏ Review daily all memory verses to date to be sure that you know them perfectly for the Scripture-memorization review at the upcoming Growing Disciples Workshop.

❑ Review final plans for the Growing Disciples Workshop so you can share them with group members.

DURING THE SESSION

PART 1 (45/60 minutes)

Introduction (20/25 minutes)
1. Ask members to share the names of non-Christian friends they made during the past week. Ask them to write all names on their Prayer-Covenant Lists as members share what they know about their new friends. Let each person share before you lead a time of prayer for all. If some members failed to make new friends, ask everyone to pray that God will lead these members to non-Christians they can befriend.

2. Pray for the lost friends who have been mentioned. Ask members to pray for these people by name during the week. Read the promise in Matthew 18:19.

3. Ask, How are you doing with your Scripture memorization? What problems are you having? Share a challenge that you have had in this area. Review "How to Memorize Scripture" (member book, p. 112). Encourage members to continue to work on this process and to pray for God's guidance.

4. Ask members to work in pairs to check each other's "My Walk with the Master This Week" and share an insight from the Daily Master Communication Guide.

"Witness to the World" (25/30 minutes)
Choose from the following list appropriate questions and activities for your group's study. Do not exceed the time allowance.

5. Ask, Will a volunteer please share an experience of trying to rely on your own strength as you share Christ with other people rather than relying on the Holy Spirit to empower you? Tell of your experience in this area.

6. Ask members why they believe that giving a verbal witness in addition to having Christlike traits in their lives is important.

7. Call for a volunteer to tell about a time when someone's comment about a positive trait seen in the person provided an opportunity for a verbal witness.

8. Ask each member to choose one of the fruit of the Spirit mentioned in Galatians 5:22-23 and tell how it can become the basis of a verbal witness (see member book, pp. 93-94).

9. Ask members to describe excuses they have made for not witnessing. Share one of the excuses you have made in the past.

10. Ask, Will someone please tell about a time that Jesus worked so powerfully in your life that you could not help but tell what you had experienced? Allow two or three members to respond.

11. Ask volunteers to share where they believe they are in their readiness to testify about what Christ has done in their lives.

P9
108
12. Read aloud John 15:20-21. Ask members how they feel about the fact that bearing fruit for Christ has its price. Ask for a volunteer to share about a price he or she has paid for being a Christian.

13. Ask members to recall the types of suffering Jesus encountered other than the ones listed on page 108 in the member book. Remind members that Jesus was the only sinless person who has ever lived; His suffering was completely undeserved.

14. Close this part of the session by asking members to pray for the person on their right. Ask God to help this person bear fruit by learning to give a verbal witness for Christ.

Take a stand-up break. Invite participants to help themselves to refreshments.

PART 2 (45/60 minutes)

The Disciple's Cross (20/30 minutes)
1. Ask members to get in pairs to check each other's presentation of the Disciple's Cross so far. Members likely will have mastered the center circle and the vertical and horizontal bars. Remind them that they will need to present the complete Disciple's Cross in their own words in next week's session so each person is signed off on this presentation before the Growing Disciples Workshop. In checking off the presentation, each person will be asked to quote all the verses that accompany the Disciple's Cross.

Next Week's Assignments (20/25 minutes)
2. Describe the upcoming Growing Disciples Workshop. Explain its purpose.

3. Ask members to look at "My Walk with the Master This Week" for week 6 on page 114 and preview the specific assignments. Make sure they understand how to complete each assignment. Urge them to complete all assignments before the Growing Disciples Workshop. At the workshop members will be asked to share with others what they have learned.

4. Briefly preview the content of week 6. Ask members to complete week 6, "Minister to Others," before session 6. Tell them it will help them minister to others as they learn to take up their crosses and follow Christ.

5. Call attention to the Discipleship Inventory on page 139 in the member book. Say, The inventory is a way to evaluate your growth in discipleship. It is based on the characteristics of a disciple. You will score and interpret your responses at the Growing Disciples Workshop. Be as honest as possible in evaluating yourself. Wait until after session 6 and before the workshop to complete the inventory.

6. Point out to members that before the Growing Disciples Workshop, they will be asked to draw something to illustrate the concepts of the Disciple's Cross. This learning activity will indicate how well they understand the truths illustrated in the Disciple's Cross. Urge them to draw the picture even if they don't believe they have artistic ability. The important thing is not the artwork but the concepts contained in it.

Closure (5 minutes)
7. Announce the time, date, and place for the Growing Disciples Workshop. Provide information about transportation to the site if the workshop is held away from your regular meeting place. Ask for volunteers to provide rides for others, if needed.

8. Close with prayer. Thank God for the progress members have made. Ask God for courage, wisdom, and efficient use of time in the week ahead to prepare for the Growing Disciples Workshop.

AFTER THE SESSION
❑ Pray for those who are struggling to keep up with the assignments. Pray that they will use their time wisely during the coming week to catch up in areas where they are behind.
❑ Ask God to guide members as they take the Discipleship Inventory. Ask Him to give them courage to be honest with their responses.
❑ Take two members with you to minister or to witness. Perhaps you can visit some of the persons on their Prayer-Covenant Lists.
❑ Make final arrangements for the Growing Disciples Workshop. Contact the meeting site to confirm arrangements for food, meeting

space, and other matters. Arrange for any materials you need for the workshop.

❑ Send an invitation to each member listing the time, date, and place of the Growing Disciples Workshop (see sample below).

---

*In acknowledgment of your walk with the Master
and to celebrate your completion of*
MasterLife 1: The Disciple's Cross,
*you are cordially invited
to attend a
Growing Disciples Workshop.
(time • date • place)*

*Please bring your book indicating your completed assignments and
your completed Discipleship Inventory.*

Enclose a map if the workshop will be held away from your regular meeting site. Furnish a phone number where members could be reached in an emergency. Provide other instructions if members are to bring a sack lunch or snacks.

❑ Read "Before the Session" for week 6 to evaluate the amount of time you will need to prepare for your next group session. At the top of the week 6 material record when you will prepare.

❑ Begin to preview *MasterLife 2: The Disciple's Personality*. You will preview book 2 for members during the Growing Disciples Workshop.

Split-Session Plan

FIRST WEEK
Follow part 1 of the session as suggested except for these adjustments.

1. Lead the study "Witness to the World." Review items 5-9 only. The remaining items pertain to material members will study next week.

2. Remind members to check off only those assignments pertaining to this week's material. Other assignments will be done the following week. Preview the assignments they will be responsible for next week.

SECOND WEEK
Follow the Standard Plan for part 2 of the session with the following exceptions.

1. Pair members with persons other than their spouses. Each member of the pair should check the other person's "My Walk with the Master This Week." The boxes with the vertical marks should be verified and marked with horizontal lines. John 15:8 should be quoted accurately by each member before that assignment is marked off.

2. Lead the study "Witness to the World." Spend about three minutes reviewing what members learned during the first week in this study. Ask for volunteers to summarize important points from last week. Then move on to items 10-14 in part 1.

3. Preview next week's assignments. Assign days 1-3 in week 6, "Minister to Others." Members are to complete only assignments that pertain to the material they study this week. Remind members that the complete Disciple's Cross should be presented and checked off by the end of the book.

One-to-One Plan

Follow instructions in the Standard Plan. Spend time on the Disciple's Cross by letting your partner give the presentation to you. Affirm his or her work and encourage further mastery of the material.

GROUP SESSION 6

Minister to Others

Session Goals

By the end of this session, members will be able to demonstrate their progress toward *MasterLife* goals by ...

- sharing how they have seen other group members grow during *MasterLife;*
- reporting the kind acts they did for their new non-Christian friends;
- completing assignments for week 6;
- explaining what "take up your cross" means to them personally;
- completing memorization work on the Disciple's Cross;
- preparing for the Growing Disciples Workshop.

Standard Plan

BEFORE THE SESSION
❑ Review week 6 of *MasterLife 1: The Disciple's Cross.*
❑ Pray daily for each member of your group.
❑ Master this week's material in the leader guide.
❑ Review the goals for this session.
❑ Check with the host or hostess to be sure he or she is ready for the group this week.
❑ Arrange the meeting place so that members can sit in a circle.
❑ Have pens or pencils and extra blank paper on hand for the session.
❑ Review any last-minute plans you have made for the Growing Disciples Workshop and share them with group members.

DURING THE SESSION

PART 1 (45/60 minutes)

Introduction (10/15 minutes)
1. Greet members. Ask them to share one change they have seen in the person seated to their right since beginning *MasterLife.*

2. Ask each person to thank God for his or her progress in *MasterLife* and for the progress that the person to his or her left has mentioned.

Verifying Assignments (10/15 minutes)
3. Ask each member to pair up with another member to check assignments for book 1. Encourage everyone to have assignments completely checked off by the end of this session. If a member needs a few minutes to complete an assignment, arrange to meet with that person during break or after the session. Ask members to get together to check any other incomplete assignments before the Growing Disciples Workshop.

"Minister to Others" (25/30 minutes)
Choose from the following list the appropriate questions and activities for your group's study. Do not exceed the time allowance.

4. Ask members to describe situations in which they have had opportunities to serve someone sacrificially (member book, p. 115). Ask members if they can remember opportunities they encountered but did not pursue. Allow two or three people to share with the group.

5. Say, Describe what cross bearing means to you. Ask, What does Jesus' command to "take up your cross" mean to you personally?

Is cross bearing a burden?

✳ 6. Ask for volunteers to describe specific, personal ways they might use the following resources in the ministries listed with each one.
- The resource of the Word in the ministry of teaching. Pg 119
- The resource of prayer in the ministry of worship and intercession. 120
- The resource of fellowship in the ministry of nurture. ~~122~~ 122
- The resource of witness in the ministry of evangelism. What is evangelism? 124
- The resources of fellowship and witness in the ministry of service. #28

7. Invite a volunteer to share about a time when he or she prayed regularly for a pastor or church-staff member.

✳ 8. Ask, How do you feel when you realize Christ has said you will experience rejection when you witness in His name? How do you feel when /27 you realize Christ has promised to send the Holy Spirit to help you?

✳ 9. Share about a time when the Holy Spirit made you bold and gave you strength to minister to others. Then ask group members to tell about their experiences in this area.

✳ 10. Ask group members to discuss how they would stay connected to the Vine if their Bibles and the opportunity to pray to and worship God 131 freely were taken away.

✳ 11. As time permits ask members to select and read a portion of John 15 and tell in their own words what it means to them.

12. Close this part of the session by inviting members to pray. Say, Voice a sentence prayer for yourself. Ask God to help you find ways to use the resources you have available through Him.

Take a stand-up break. Invite participants to help themselves to refreshments.

PART 2 (45/60 minutes)

Contacts with Non-Christian Friends (10 minutes)
1. Ask members to report on any kind acts they did last week for their new non-Christian friends. Encourage each person to participate.

2. Pray for the lost friends who have been mentioned. Pray that the group members' kind acts will be entry points for sharing the gospel when the time is appropriate.

The Disciple's Cross (15/20 minutes)
3. Instruct members to get in pairs to check each other's presentation of the Disciple's Cross. Remind members who are not checked off to

arrange to meet with another group member during the week to present the Disciple's Cross. Each person needs to be signed off on this presentation before the Growing Disciples Workshop. In checking off the presentation, each person will be asked to quote all the verses that accompany the Disciple's Cross.

Next Week's Assignments (15/20 minutes)
4. Ask, Do you have any questions about the Growing Disciples Workshop? Distribute maps and other information as needed.

5. Urge members who may not yet have completed all their assignments to work to finish them before the Growing Disciples Workshop. At the workshop, members will be asked to share what they have learned.

6. Remind members about the Discipleship Inventory on pages 139-43 in the member book. Ask everyone to complete it before the workshop. They will score and interpret their responses at the workshop. Encourage members to be honest when completing the inventory.

7. Point out that at the Growing Disciples Workshop members will be asked to share and explain the things they have drawn to illustrate the concepts of the Disciple's Cross (p. 133). The learning activity will indicate how well they understand the truths illustrated in the Disciple's Cross.

Remind them this is not an art contest; the important thing is the concepts contained in the picture.

Closure (5/10 minutes)
8. Refresh members' memories about the time, date, and place for the Growing Disciples Workshop. Finalize transportation if needed.

9. Close with prayer. Ask God to help members as they prepare to complete their work on *MasterLife 1: The Disciple's Cross.*

AFTER THE SESSION
❑ Pray for those who are struggling to complete assignments. Pray they will use their time wisely to finish incomplete areas.
❑ Ask God to guide members as they take the Discipleship Inventory. Ask God to give them courage to be honest with their responses.
❑ Take two members with you to minister or to witness.
❑ Make final arrangements for the Growing Disciples Workshop. Contact the meeting site to confirm arrangements. Secure materials you need for the workshop.
❑ Read the plans for the Growing Disciples Workshop to evaluate the amount of final preparation you will need.

❏ Review *MasterLife 2: The Disciple's Personality* and be prepared to give a brief overview at the Growing Disciples Workshop.

Split-Session Plan

1. For the first week follow part 1 of the session as it is outlined in the Standard Plan. Lead the study "Minister to Others." Review items 4-7 only.

2. For the second week follow part 2 of the session, including items 8-11 from part 1.

3. Each week spend time discussing questions members might have about the Growing Disciples Workshop. The Growing Disciples Workshop is not designed for a split session.

One-to-One Plan

Follow the Standard Plan as you work with your partner. Spend extra time answering questions about the Growing Disciples Workshop and the Discipleship Inventory. Share any experiences you have had in taking the inventory and insights it gave you about your life. Pray a prayer of thanksgiving for your partner's growth in *MasterLife*.

Growing Disciples Workshop

Note to those using the Split-Session Plan and the One-to-One Plan: The *Split-Session Plan* is not appropriate for this workshop. The workshop should be scheduled at a time when three uninterrupted hours can be devoted to it. The workshop lends itself to the *One-to-One Plan.* For example, spend extra time helping the individual process his or her Discipleship Inventory. Ask the individual to explain his or her Disciple's Cross concept diagram and you as leader explain the one you have drawn. Ask the individual to share about changes in his or her life during *MasterLife;* pray a prayer of thanksgiving for the changes mentioned.

Workshop Goals

By the end of this workshop, members will be able to demonstrate their progress toward *MasterLife* goals by ...

- sharing how they have seen themselves grow during *MasterLife;*
- completing all assignments in *MasterLife 1: The Disciple's Cross;*
- explaining their diagram that illustrates the concepts of the Disciple's Cross;
- completing the Discipleship Inventory and evaluating the results;
- examining ways they plan to seek continued growth in Christ.

BEFORE THE WORKSHOP

- ❏ Review the basic content of *MasterLife 2: The Disciple's Personality* so you can give an overview at the Growing Disciples Workshop.
- ❏ Pray daily for each member of your group.
- ❏ Call each member of the group to be sure everyone will be there.
- ❏ Master the material in this leader guide for the Growing Disciples Workshop.
- ❏ Review the goals for the workshop.
- ❏ Check with the persons responsible for the meeting site to be sure they are ready for the group.

- ❏ Arrange the meeting place so that members can sit in a circle.
- ❏ Choose either to show the video presentation of the Disciple's Personality or to make the presentation yourself. If you choose to present the material yourself, preview the way Avery Willis does it on the videotape. Then develop your own script. If you choose to show the video, secure video equipment and cue the tape before the session begins.
- ❏ Make enough copies of "Scoring Your Inventory" (pp. 67-70) for each member to have one.
- ❏ Have pens or pencils and extra blank paper on hand for the workshop.
- ❏ Make plans for starting the study of *MasterLife 2: The Disciple's Personality.* Arrange a time, date, and place for the first meeting. Be prepared to share these plans with group members. Have books on hand at the workshop for members to purchase.
- ❏ Pray for the workshop. Members need to have a sense of accomplishment and success at the end of *MasterLife 1: The Disciple's Cross.* They will get this from having all their work in "My Walk with the Master This Week" checked off and by assessing their growth as disciples.
- ❏ Prepare the following as a printed agenda to be distributed, or write it on a poster or chalkboard.

Today's Workshop Agenda
- The Disciple's Cross
- Discipleship Inventory
- The Disciple's Personality

DURING THE WORKSHOP

PART 1 (60 minutes)

Icebreaker (5 minutes)

1. Greet members. Ask each person to share one change he or she has seen in himself or herself since beginning *MasterLife.* Go around the group until each member has responded.

2. Pray, asking each person to thank God for the progress in *MasterLife* that he or she has observed in group members' lives.

The Disciple's Cross (45 minutes)

3. Ask each member to show and describe his or her diagram that illustrates the concepts of the Disciple's Cross. Tell each person to quote the Scriptures that accompany each part of the cross, as illustrated by their diagram.

4. Affirm each member's presentation after he or she finishes. Ask questions about the presentation to show interest, and encourage other members to comment or ask questions they might have. Take care to affirm each member regardless of the degree of artistic ability displayed in the drawings.

5. Post the illustrations in a prominent place in the room so everyone can enjoy them. Leave them on display the remainder of the workshop. Encourage members to study each diagram carefully.

6. Consider displaying the illustrations in a prominent place in your church after the workshop. Accompany the display with a note explaining that these illustrations are an outgrowth of the Growing Disciples Workshop. This type of display provides visual interest and serves as good promotion to attract prospective *MasterLife* members in your church.

Verifying Assignments (10 minutes)

7. Ask each member to pair up with another member. If any member still needs a few minutes to complete an assignment for book 1, such as memorizing a Scripture, take time to do this now. If both members of the pair have all their assignments checked off, use this time to practice reviewing the Scriptures they have memorized in book 1. Arrange to meet at break time with anyone who still needs to have an assignment checked off.

Break (15 minutes)

PART 2 (45 minutes)

Discipleship Inventory (45 minutes)

1. Ask members to turn to the Discipleship Inventory on page 139 in their member books. Ask them how they felt as they took the inventory. Say, The Discipleship Inventory is based on the characteristics of a disciple and attempts to help you determine where you are in your growth as a disciple.

2. Distribute copies of "Scoring Your Inventory." Allow sufficient time for members to score their inventories. Be available to answer questions.

3. Debrief what members discovered about themselves from the inventory. Discuss each of the five categories one by one using the ideas below as starters. Avoid embarrassing members by asking their scores; some will volunteer this information.
• **Attitude** Ask, Does the list under "Attitude" on page 70 contain any characteristics that you do not think a disciple should have? Are there characteristics you would add? Which characteristic is most difficult to exemplify?
• **Behavior** Say, People often find that their attitudes are better than their behavior. Look at your scores for each of these two categories. Ask, Do you see a wide range of difference? Which is higher? What does that say to you about their relationship in your life?
• **Relationships** Ask, How do you relate to God based on the inventory? How do you relate to others? How important is the fellowship of other Christians? Ask a volunteer to comment on one characteristic he or she would like to improve.
• **Ministry** Ask, How important is it for a disciple to minister to others? What Scriptures encourage or expect ministry from Christ's disciples? Did you find your score in attitude and behavior better than in ministry? If so, what does this suggest?
• **Doctrine** Ask, Are there doctrines listed that you do not agree are taught in the Bible? (Be careful not to let this become a theological debate.) Ask, How can we live lives that demonstrate our beliefs?

4. Discuss levels expected. Remind members that they will take the inventory again at the end of book 4 so they can identify areas in which they have grown.

5. Discuss how the next three books in the *MasterLife* series will meet specific needs in this growth process. Read Philippians 3:12-14 and encourage members to fulfill Paul's goal.

Break (10 minutes)

PART 3 (50 minutes)

The Disciple's Personality (45 minutes)
1. Give the Disciple's Personality presentation in your own words or show the videotape.

2. Preview *MasterLife 2: The Disciple's Personality* by reviewing the weekly titles and giving a five-minute overview of the content. Lead members to decide whether to begin the sessions next week or take a week off before beginning.

3. Ask for volunteers to give personal testimonies about why they are committed to continuing the *MasterLife* study.

4. Distribute copies of *MasterLife 2: The Disciple's Personality* for those who know they want to continue in *MasterLife*. Make arrangements for other members who need to pray about continuing to call you with their decisions during the week. Announce to these members how they may pick up their copies of book 2. Assure group members that regardless of what they decide about continuing, you will always be available to talk to or pray with them about life in Christ.

5. Lead a prayer for group members, asking them to commit to the Father their decisions about whether to continue in a study of book 2. Ask God to speak clearly to them about His will for them in this matter.

Closure (5 minutes)
6. Congratulate members on completing *MasterLife 1: The Disciple's Cross*. Assure them that the time investment they have made in learning to be a follower of Christ will make their pilgrimage more meaningful in the days ahead. Express appreciation for each member.

7. Close with prayer. Invite each member to pray, thanking God for walking side by side with him or her through *MasterLife 1: The Disciple's Cross*.

AFTER THE WORKSHOP
❏ Write a note to each member expressing appreciation for his or her participation in the course. Remind each member that you are praying as he or she continues to apply concepts of *MasterLife 1: The Disciple's Cross* to daily life.

❏ Finalize your plans for beginning *MasterLife 2: The Disciple's Personality*. Confirm the meeting site. Post a notice in the church on a bulletin board or in the church newsletter to announce the formation of the *MasterLife 2: The Disciple's Personality* group. Occasionally someone who completed book 1 earlier than your group but who has never studied book 2 will want to join your group. This type of announcement makes such people aware of your group's availability.

❏ If some group members have not contacted you to make you aware of their decision about continuing *MasterLife*, telephone them to inquire about their plans. Remind them that you will be available to them and will continue to pray for them regardless of their decision. If a member informs you that he or she is declining to participate at this time, suggest that the person may want to join another group of book 1 graduates who move into book 2 at a later date.

❏ This is a good time to take stock of the leadership you provided during *MasterLife 1: The Disciple's Cross*. If you believe that a problem exists between you and one of the members, visit with this person and seek reconciliation.

❏ Spend time in prayer for each member.

❏ Seek ways through publications and gatherings of members to inform the church of the progress of the group and your expectations for them by the end of the *MasterLife* training. You may want members to share brief testimonies about what *MasterLife* has meant to them. Announce that you are accepting the names of persons who want to begin the process and enroll in *MasterLife 1: The Disciple's Cross*.

Scoring Your Inventory [1]

The Discipleship Inventory discerns strengths and weaknesses in your discipleship development. You will access your discipleship development by transferring your responses to five categories: attitudes, behavior, relationships, ministry, and doctrine.

Taking the inventory once is valuable because it gives you a beginning point for growth. Knowing where you are in each category allows you to determine the areas you need to work on. The inventory becomes even more valuable when you complete it again after a period of time. That is why we encourage you to use it at the end of books 1 and 4 in *MasterLife*. Comparing your scores in each of the five categories will indicate your degree of growth. The combined score will provide an indicator of total growth. Use the following directions to score your inventory.

1. Transfer your responses from the inventory to the scoring chart on the following two pages. Some questions are reverse-response questions. These questions are noted with an asterisk on the scoring chart. When tabulating the scores for questions 13, 20, 31, 36, 40, 56, 58, 60, 61, 65, and 84, the score should be reversed: 5=1, 4=2, 3=3, 2=4, 1=5. Numbers 136-141 and 143-152 are not required for scoring.
2. Add the values of your responses for each category and write the number in the blank labeled "Total." Divide by the number indicated and write the number in the box.
3. To calculate your combined total, add the "Totals" for each category (not the numbers in the boxes) and divide by 150. Write your combined total in the box provided.
4. On the chart below, shade each bar graph to represent your total for each category. Shade the combined-total bar to picture your overall score. Categories in which you made low scores are areas for growth in discipleship.
5. Review the descriptions on page 70 for each of the five categories. These brief summaries identify areas you might consider working on to further your growth in discipleship.

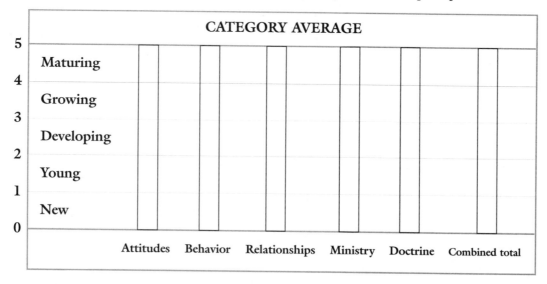

[1]Steve McCord, James Slack, and Emily Yeatts, "The Discipleship Inventory" (Richmond: The International Mission Board of the Southern Baptist Convention). Used and adapted by permission.

Discipleship Inventory

Attitudes	Behavior	Relationships	Ministry	Doctrine
1_____	1_____			
	2_____			
3_____			4_____	
		5_____		
6_____		6_____	7_____	
			8_____	
			9_____	
10_____		11_____	12_____	
		12_____		
		13_____ *		
		14_____		
		15_____		
			16_____	
17_____		17_____	18_____	
		19_____		
		20_____ *	21_____	
		22_____		
		23_____		
		24_____		
		25_____		
		26_____	26_____	
			27_____	
				28_____
29_____		30_____		
			32_____	31_____ *
33_____			34_____	
				35_____
36_____ *				37_____
				38_____
			39_____	
				40_____ *
	41_____		41_____	
	42_____		43_____	
			44_____	
	45_____			
	46_____			
	47_____			
	48_____			
49_____		50_____		
		51_____		
		52_____		
		53_____		
	54_____	54_____		
	55_____			
		56_____ *		
		57_____		
	58_____ *		58_____ *	
	59_____			
		60_____ *		
		61_____ *		
	62_____			
		63_____		
		64_____		
			65_____ *	
	66_____			
	67_____			
	68_____			
	69_____			
		70_____		

Attitudes	Behavior	Relationships	Ministry	Doctrine
		71_____	72_____	
			73_____	
		74_____	75_____	
			76_____	
			77_____	
			78_____	
			79_____	
80_____	80_____			
81_____				
82_____				82_____
83_____		84_____ *		
			85_____	
87_____				86_____
	88_____	89_____		
				90_____
				91_____
			92_____	
			93_____	
			94_____	
			95_____	
			96_____	
			97_____	
	99_____	98_____		
		100_____		
		102_____	101_____	
		103_____		
	104_____			
		106_____	105_____	
			107_____	
			108_____	
	110_____	109_____		
111_____				
113_____		112_____		
		113_____		
115_____			114_____	
116_____				
117_____				
118_____			118_____	
119_____				
120_____			120_____	
		121_____		
		122_____		
		123_____		
		124_____		
		125_____		
		126_____		126_____
				127_____
				128_____
				129_____
				130_____
				131_____
				132_____
				133_____
				134_____
				135_____
				142_____

Attitudes	Behavior	Relationships	Ministry	Doctrine	
Total _____ +	_____ +	_____ +	_____ +	_____ =	_____
Divide by 22=	Divide by 22=	Divide by 46=	Divide by 39=	Divide by 21=	Divide by 150=
☐	☐	☐	☐	☐	☐

Categories in the Discipleship Inventory

ATTITUDES

A disciple …

- possesses a desire and willingness to learn.
- lives according to biblical principles and guidelines.
- repents after violating Scripture.
- forfeits personal desires and conveniences, if necessary, to meet the needs of others.
- practices humility (transparent and honest about weaknesses).
- lives a life of integrity (personal life matches public image).
- is accountable to others.

BEHAVIOR

A disciple …

- utilizes time and talent for God's purposes.
- adapts attitudes and actions to conform to biblical standards.
- acts appropriately toward the opposite sex.

RELATIONSHIPS

A disciple …

- accepts and values himself or herself as created in the image of God.
- experiences an awareness of God's presence through the ministry of the Holy Spirit.
- trusts God in times of adversity, as well as in times of prosperity.
- seeks to commune with and learn about God by hearing, reading, studying, memorizing God's Word, and through regular prayer.
- consistently fellowships with other believers in the context of a local church.
- builds meaningful relationships with other believers beyond his or her local church.
- maintains a forgiving spirit when wronged.
- confesses or asks forgiveness when guilty of an offense.

MINISTRY

A disciple …

- publicly identifies with Christ and with the church when given the opportunity.
- seeks and takes advantage of opportunities to share the gospel with others.
- ministers to other believers.
- seeks the good of all people through a willingness to meet practical needs.

DOCTRINE

A disciple …

- believes that each person inherited a sinful nature as a result of Adam's fall and is separated from God and in need of a Savior.
- believes that God fully revealed Himself through His Son, Jesus Christ, who died for the sins of the world, was raised from the dead, and will personally come a second time.
- trusts only and totally in Christ for salvation.
- experiences the Holy Spirit's complete entrance at the time of the new birth.
- looks to Jesus Christ for eternal security.
- accepts and follows the Bible as the authoritative and completely reliable revelation of God.
- believes that the church is God's means for nurturing believers, preserving doctrine, and carrying out His plan for propagating the gospel.
- believes that heaven is the final abode of believers and that hell is the final abode of all who have never accepted Jesus Christ as Savior.

THE DISCIPLE'S PERSONALITY

MasterLife

BOOK 2

"I have come that they may have life, and have it to the full" (John 10:10).

God will use *The Disciple's Personality* to lead group members
to develop Christlikeness in character as they learn to live in the Spirit.

Contents

INTRODUCTORY SESSION

How to Have Life in the Spirit

Conduct this Introductory Session before your group members study week 1 of *MasterLife 2: The Disciple's Personality* if you are leading a group that has not studied *MasterLife 1: The Disciple's Cross*. If your group is moving directly from *MasterLife 1: The Disciple's Cross*, skip the Introductory Session and move directly to Group Session 1.

Consider conducting this session if a substantial amount of time has elapsed between *MasterLife 1: The Disciple's Cross* and beginning this study, or if your group did not have sufficient time at the Growing Disciple's Workshop to cover the presentation of the Disciple's Personality and other previews of book 2.

Note to those using the Split-Session Plan: No matter where you begin, the Split-Session Plan begins with Group Session 2. Assignments for session 2 are in Group Session 1 plans.

Session Goals
By the end of this session, members will be able to demonstrate their commitment to *MasterLife* by ...
- telling at least one piece of information about each group member;
- explaining the general concepts of a drawing of the Disciple's Cross;
- explaining the general concepts of the Disciple's Personality;
- doing the assignments for week 1.

Standard Plan

BEFORE THE SESSION
❑ Review the introduction and complete the learning activities for week 1 of *MasterLife 2: The Disciple's Personality* in order to stay ahead of the group. At the end of this session you will preview week 1 for the members.
❑ Find a quiet time and place to pray for group members by name. Ask the Lord to give you the wisdom to prepare for and lead the group session.
❑ Read "During the Session."

8. Offer to help members as they develop in discipleship by spending time with the Master, living in the Word, praying in faith, fellowshipping with believers, witnessing to the world, and ministering to others. Explain that they will have assignments in these categories each week. Say, The Disciple's Cross will help you in several ways.

- You will know the six disciplines of Christ's disciple.
- You will experience each of the six disciplines as it functions in your life each day.
- You will be able to use the disciplines as a standard to remind you and to help other Christians see the commitments required for being Christ's disciple.
- These disciplines will help you follow the direction of the Holy Spirit as you deal with problems in your Christian life.
- You will be able to help other disciples live in Christ and bear fruit for His glory.

9. Explain how the Disciple's Cross relates to the Disciple's Personality. Say, The circle in the center of the Disciple's Cross represents you—your total personality, a unity. The circle you draw represents you. You will come to understand during this study why you act the way you do.

Take a stand-up break. Invite participants to help themselves to refreshments.

PART 2 (35/50 minutes)

Prayer Time (5 minutes)
1. Ask each member to pair with another person, preferably not their spouse. Invite members to share with the other person a concern they have in their lives. Instruct them to pray for each other's needs.

The Disciple's Personality (15/20 minutes)
2. Ask members to tell you what the circle in the Disciple's Cross represents. *(You,* or *Christ in you.)* Tell them that you want to expand that circle to show how they can make Christ the Lord of their total personalities.

3. Give the Disciple's Personality presentation on page 133 in the member book or view the video presentation. Before either showing the video or making the presentation yourself, provide each member three blank sheets of paper to copy the three drawings demonstrated during the presentation. If you make the presentation, present it as you would in a spontaneous, informal setting. Draw it on the chalkboard or on newsprint as you would draw it on a paper napkin or a piece of paper. Explain that members will master the Disciple's Personality a section at a time over a four-week period.

Week 1 Assignments (10/20 minutes)

4. Ask members to look in their member books on page 8 at "My Walk with the Master This Week." Instruct them to review the specific assignments. Say, As you complete an assignment, you will draw a vertical line through the diamond. A fellow member verifying your work during the first group session will draw a horizontal line through the diamond to form a cross.

5. Preview the content of week 1 briefly. Ask members to complete the activities in week 1, "Do God's Will," before Group Session 1. Call attention to two important elements in their study. Say,

- You will be encouraged to spend time with a family member. This may be a family member with whom you have not talked in a while. Write or call if this person lives far away. Christians often neglect to spend time with persons closest to them even as they minister to others within their sphere of influence.
- If you did not participate in *MasterLife 1: The Disciple's Cross*, be aware of the Prayer-Covenant List. This assignment directs you to list the names of five people you need to witness to. Look at a copy of the Prayer-Covenant List on page 143 of the member book. You will record on your lists names, dates, and answers to prayers. You are asked to do this as you begin to think of five people who need a witness.

Closure (5 minutes)

6. Announce the time and place for the next meeting.

7. Ask the group to stand and join hands for a prayer of dismissal. Invite each member to voice a one-sentence prayer for the person seated to his or her left, especially as that person begins to think about five people who do not know Christ.

8. Express gratitude for each member and ask them to pray for you as you seek to lead them in the days ahead.

AFTER THE SESSION

❏ Before the next group session pray for each member specifically.

❏ Call each member and encourage him or her in the study of the first week's material. Answer questions they may have, and encourage any who seem to need it. Thank each member for his or her commitment to the group.

❏ If anyone expresses doubt about joining the *MasterLife* group permanently, consider others to take their place. Ask anyone new joining the group to complete the study "Do God's Will" before the next session. They will easily be able to start week 1. New members should not join the group after the next session.

❑ Use the following questions to evaluate your leadership.
  • Was I thoroughly prepared?
  • Was my presentation clear?
  • Did I follow the leader guide?
  • Did I provide positive leadership?
  • Was I a 2 Timothy 2:24-25 type leader?
  • Was I an enabler?
  • Did I create a group environment?
  • Did I help members communicate with each other?
  • Do members understand the purpose of the study?
  • Was I enthusiastic about how God will use *MasterLife* in members' lives and our church?

❑ Read "Before the Session" for the first group session to evaluate the amount of preparation you will need. At the top of the first page of Group Session 1 material, record when you will prepare.

❑ Carefully study week 2 and do all the exercises in the member book. You will preview week 2 for members during session 1.

One-to-One Study Plan

PART 1

1. Follow directions for the Standard Plan during the introductory time. Use this opportunity to discover needs and to help meet them. Allow the person to interact and ask questions to discover answers as you talk together rather than your monopolizing the conversation. Be a friend.

2. Follow the Standard Plan for giving an overview of the material in *MasterLife 2: The Disciple's Personality* and for presenting the Disciple's Cross. Share how you have used the Disciple's Cross in your own life.

PART 2

Present the material related to the Disciple's Personality. Explain that he or she will not learn the presentation all at one time but will add new material each week. The member will be expected to present the Disciple's Personality in his or her own words at the end of the study. If you have used the Disciple's Personality, tell how you used it and share the benefits. Follow the Standard Plan for explaining the first week's assignments.

GROUP SESSION 1

Do God's Will

Session Goals

By the end of this session, members will be able to demonstrate their commitment to *MasterLife* by ...

- stating goals for their study of *MasterLife 2: The Disciple's Personality;*
- explaining the Natural Person part of the Disciple's Personality;
- praying for lost friends that group members have named;
- saying from memory Philippians 2:13;
- describing three requirements for doing God's will;
- completing the assignments for week 1.

Standard Plan

BEFORE THE SESSION

❑ Review the introduction and complete the learning activities for week 1 of *MasterLife 2: The Disciple's Personality* in order to conduct this week's group activities.

❑ Study week 2 and do the exercises in the member book. You will preview week 2 for the group at the end of this session.

❑ Find a quiet time and place to pray for group members by name. Ask the Lord to give you wisdom to prepare and lead the group session.

❑ Read "During the Session."

❑ Have at least five lost persons on your Prayer-Covenant List and be prepared to discuss this activity with group members.

❑ Arrange for refreshments to be served at the beginning of the session or at the break.

❑ Arrange in a circle chairs for everyone in the group.

❑ Have pens or pencils and extra blank paper on hand for the session.

❑ Plan to stay within the times given for each part. You may want to print an agenda with the subjects and times listed. This will guide the group and allow members to help the group stay on schedule.

Remember that allowing members to share freely is far more important than sticking legalistically to a plan you develop for the group session. Group members sometimes arrive at a session eager to tell about something that happened in their lives during the week related to that week's content. Be sensitive to this need, and be flexible. Allow God to work in your group. Provide opportunities for everyone to respond during the session.

DURING THE SESSION

PART 1 (45/60 minutes)

Introduction (10/15 minutes)
1. Welcome each person and point them to the refreshments. As leader, express genuine interest in members as they arrive. Express to each person how glad you are they are participating in the *MasterLife* study. Let everyone visit informally until time to begin.

2. Begin promptly. Remind the group that you will begin and end each session on time. If group members want to fellowship or talk after the sessions, they may do so, but they can count on you to be prompt.

3. If your group members were together for *MasterLife 1: The Disciple's Cross* and did not participate in the introductory session, give a brief overview of the course goals for *MasterLife 2: The Disciple's Personality.* If they participated in the introductory session, skip the overview.

4. Ask members to sign the covenant for this study on page 7. If members did not participate in *MasterLife 1: The Disciple's Cross* and are starting with book 2, explain the purpose and importance of the covenant.

5. Ask each member to give a one-sentence statement of his or her goals for this course. Call the group to prayer. Ask members to say a sentence prayer asking God to help them achieve their goals.

"Do God's Will" (30/40 minutes)
Choose from the following list appropriate questions and activities for your group. Watch your time.

6. Ask, How does God's will differ from a person's will? (See the answer on p. 11.) Why does God want you to do His will? What is His primary purpose for your life? *(To bring glory to God. Many other reasons may be given, but they all bring glory to God.)*

7. Ask, How did Jesus fulfill His vision of God's purpose for His life? *(He died to redeem humanity.)* Ask volunteers to state their vision of God's purpose for their lives.

8. Ask one member to share his or her answer to the first activity in day 3. Discuss the difficulties in doing God's will. Then ask, How does God provide the resources for doing His will?

"In the Carpenter's Shop" (5 minutes)
9. Ask a volunteer to sum up some of the tendencies of the old life. Ask another volunteer to sum up some of the tendencies of the new life.

Close in prayer, asking God to help members develop Christlike character during this study.

Take a stand-up break. Invite participants to help themselves to refreshments.

PART 2 (45/60 minutes)

Prayer Time (5 minutes)
1. Ask each member to pair with another person, preferably not their spouse. Say, Briefly summarize your experiences this week. Share with your partner the names of five lost persons on your prayer list. Pray for the people on your partner's list.

Presentation: The Natural Person (15/20 minutes)
2. Remind group members that they are expanding the circle in the center of the Disciple's Cross to show how they can make Christ the Lord of their total personalities. Give a brief overview of the Disciple's Personality presented at the Growing Disciples Workshop.

3. Instruct each person to present to another person in his or her own words the Natural Person part of the Disciple's Personality. If they give the majority of the ideas correctly, the partner should draw an upright line in the diamond on "Minister to Others" in "My Walk with the Master This Week." Members are not expected to have learned the rest of the presentation. The Disciple's Personality is to be mastered a section at a time over a four-week period. Encourage them to use any extra time to check on other assignments. If several of the members did not give most of the ideas correctly in this presentation, consider showing the video presentation of the Disciple's Personality or loaning it to them to refresh their memories.

Discussion: The Natural Person (5/10 minutes)
4. Ask volunteers to share answers to the following questions:
• What causes you to inherit a nature that is inclined toward sin?
• Why can't good deeds alone cause a person in the flesh to please God?
• What happens when the big *I* in your personality takes over in your life?
• What part of your personality gives additional evidence that you were created in the image of God?

Principles of Conversational Prayer (15 minutes)
5. Introduce conversational prayer. Say, The most common mistakes are using *us* and *we;* moving to a new subject before everyone has had a chance to pray about the current subject; using formal terms of address

for God; and not praying short prayers. Ask members to pray conversationally in groups of four. After they finish, tell them that they will review "Principles of Conversational Prayer" in next week's lesson.

Next Week's Assignments (5/10 minutes)
6. Ask members to look at "My Walk with the Master This Week" for week 2 and review the specific assignments. Remind them again that as they complete an assignment, they will draw a vertical line through the diamond. A fellow member will verify their work during session 2 and draw a horizontal line through the diamond to form a cross.

7. Preview the content of week 2 briefly. Ask members to complete the activities in "Renew Your Mind" before next week's session. Say,
- You will be asked to begin having a daily quiet time 21 consecutive days. The purpose of the 21-day goal is to establish a daily quiet time as a regular pattern in your schedule.
- You will receive an assignment to go out to dinner or plan a private time with your spouse or, if you are not married, a close friend. This assignment is designed to contribute to the health of relationships within the body of Christ.
- You will also be asked to do something good for a non-Christian member of your immediate or extended family. Don't overlook unsaved family members when you are thinking about those who need the good news of Christ.

8. Elaborate on "In the Carpenter's Shop" from last week. Say, These activities, which occur several times during each week's work, are designed to help you determine ways that you need to become more like Christ.

Closure (5 minutes)
9. Close with prayer. Invite members to stand and join hands in a prayer of dismissal. Ask them to voice a one-sentence prayer for the person seated to their left, especially as that person relates to non-Christian family members during the coming week. Express gratitude that you are part of the group, and request members' prayers for you as you serve them during the weeks that follow.

AFTER THE SESSION
❑ Before the next group session pray for each member specifically.
❑ Call each group member and encourage him or her in their study. Answer any questions they may have, and encourage anyone who seems to need it. Thank group members for their commitment.
❑ Use the following questions to evaluate your leadership.
  - Was I thoroughly prepared?
  - Was my presentation clear?

- Did I follow the leader guide?
- Did I provide positive leadership?
- Was I a servant leader?
- Did I create a group environment?
- Did I help members communicate with each other?
- Do members understand the purpose of the study?
- Was I enthusiastic about how God will use *MasterLife* in members' lives and our church?

❑ Read "Before the Session" for Group Session 2 to evaluate the amount of preparation you will need. At the top of the first page of Group Session 2 material, record when you will prepare.

❑ Carefully study week 3 and do all the exercises in the member book. You will preview week 3 for members during session 2.

Split-Session Plan

1. The split-session plan begins with Group Session 2. Session 1 should be conducted as a single session.

2. Preview next week's assignment. Assign days 1-3 of the study "Renew Your Mind" for the first week of session 2 and days 4-5 for the second week of session 2.

One-to-One Study Plan

PART 1

1. Follow directions for the Standard Plan. Use your time to learn about this person and how you can best help him or her. Avoid lecturing to the person; allow him or her to discover answers as you work together.

2. Ask the person to quote Philippians 2:13, the verse he or she memorized during the week. Review "Do God's Will." Explore the person's vision of God's purpose for his or her life. Share your vision of God's purpose for your life. Share any insight you may have for the person's life. Share a Bible promise you would claim for the person. Discuss parts of your personalities that might not be fully committed to God. Read verses that help you commit each part of your personality to God.

3. Discuss the problem of doing God's will even though you are committed to Christ. Talk about the two natures people have. Discuss God's provision for helping you do His will.

4. Discuss the segment "In the Carpenter's Shop." Because you are working one-to-one, you can spend more time helping the person understand the principles of developing Christlike character. Tell about experiences in setting aside old ways and putting on new traits.

PART 2

Ask the person to present the material on the Natural Person part of the Disciple's Personality. Follow the Standard Plan for reviewing week 2 assignments.

GROUP SESSION 2

Renew Your Mind

Session Goals

By the end of this session, members will be able to demonstrate their progress toward *MasterLife* goals by …

- having a date or private time with their spouse or a close friend;
- completing assignments for week 2;
- explaining the Worldly Christian part of the *Disciple's Personality*;
- identifying ways to renew their minds and committing themselves to a course of action;
- praying, using "Principles of Conversational Prayer;"
- praying for group members' family members who do not know Christ.

Standard Plan

BEFORE THE SESSION

❑ Review week 2 and read and complete the activities for week 3 in *MasterLife 2: The Disciple's Personality.*

❑ Pray daily for each member of the group. Ask the Lord to give you wisdom to prepare for and lead the group session.

❑ Read carefully "During the Session."

❑ Review the goals for this session.

❑ Check with the host or hostess to be sure he or she is ready for the group this week.

❑ Arrange the meeting place so that members can sit in a circle.

❑ Use name tags while members are still learning each other's names.

❑ Have pens or pencils and extra blank paper on hand for the session.

❑ Be prepared to report on your date with your spouse or meal with a friend.

❑ Master "How to Listen to God's Word" on pages 59-61 in the member book so you can teach it to the group. Be prepared to refer to the Hearing the Word form (p.141) during the session.

❑ Get a 10 or 12 penny nail or a sharp pencil for each person.

❑ As you prepare to train members using "Testimony Outline" (p. 69), review your personal testimony to be sure it meets the guidelines. Be prepared to share your testimony without notes and to tell members how you prepared your testimony according to the outline provided in the member book.

❑ Begin to make plans for the Testimony Workshop that follows session 6. Ask the group the best time and place for the workshop. The workshop will last three hours. You might want to meet at some time other than in the evening. Meet at the church or at a place where members can work individually at tables while you help others in the group with their testimonies. Perhaps a Saturday morning or afternoon or a Sunday afternoon would be appropriate.

❑ Enlist someone to help you listen to testimonies as group members prepare them. This can be a respected member of your church, someone who has completed *MasterLife*, or a current group member who is demonstrating maturity in discipleship. You can train this helper by showing him or her the video segment on evaluating testimonies. Week 3 instructions will guide you in how this person can help you.

❑ Preview the videotape on testimonies. Practice evaluating the testimonies on the videotape.

❑ Review the following general instructions in your preparation.

  • Don't be critical of members who have not memorized the Scripture-memory verses word-perfect, but each week encourage them to work toward the mastery of each verse.

  • Don't reprimand those who have problems completing assignments. Praise them for what they do; ask others to share insights that might be helpful in completing assignments. Encourage members to bear each other's burdens.

DURING THE SESSION

PART 1 (45/60 minutes)

Getting Started (5 minutes)
1. Greet members as they arrive. Begin on time. Be alert to signs of progress or any problems members may be facing. Open the session with prayer. Ask for special prayer requests.

My Walk with the Master This Week (15 minutes)
2. Ask members to pair with someone other than their spouses to check "My Walk with the Master This Week." They will ask the other person if he or she did the assignment. In some cases the person verifying may ask to see the work done. Members must quote memory verses correctly before this item is marked as verified.

Private Time (10/15 minutes)
3. Divide your group in half (groups of four to six persons). Invite members in each small group to share experiences they had when they

went out to dinner or spent private time with their spouse or close friend. Ask volunteers to tell what areas of growth they saw in the relationship during this private time.

Conversational Prayer (10/20 minutes)
4. Say, Stay in your small groups and discuss the key elements of conversational prayer.

5. Ask members to share experiences they had during the week in praying conversationally with family, a friend, or a prayer partner.

6. Invite members to pray conversationally. Ask them to start praying without anyone making requests. As they mention requests in their prayers, others can pray for the same thing.

"Renew Your Mind" (20/30 minutes)
7. Remind members of the importance of completing all exercises and learning the materials before they attend the group session. The purpose for discussing the study in the group session is to reflect on it, explore the subject further, and apply it.

8. Say, In an age of mass media, Madison-Avenue advertising, and mood-control drugs, the question of who controls your mind is relevant. Does a non-Christian have a choice about who or what controls his or her mind? After several responses, call on a volunteer to read Romans 7:18-20,24. Ask, So who is in control? (*Sin is in control.*)

9. Ask, Does a Christian have a choice about who or what controls his or her mind? (*Yes, the person can choose to let God control instead of letting sin control.*) Ask members to suggest verses that support their answers. Verses might include 2 Corinthians 10:5 and Colossians 2:2. Say, Not all Christians allow God to control their minds. God may have input but not have control.

10. Use the following analogy: Sheep in Bible days were trained to respond to the voice of their shepherd. Shepherds could graze their flocks together during the day. But at night each shepherd called his flock aside. The sheep responded because they knew their master's voice. We are to be trained to respond only to the voice of God. Ask a volunteer to read John 10:2-5.

11. Ask, Does letting Christ have control of our minds mean we are giving up part of our mental or intellectual capacities? (*Since Christ is the author and sustainer of truth and reality, to be controlled by Him should increase our understanding of truth and reality.*)

12. Ask a member to read 2 Corinthians 10:5. Ask, What are some worldly imaginations or arguments that can obstruct the knowledge of God? Write members' responses on a chalkboard or something large enough for everyone to see. Responses should include secular ideas, entertainment, television, magazines, books, and pictures. Ask, How can we keep these things from obstructing our knowledge of God? After several have responded, ask, What are some positive ways you can make your thoughts obedient to Christ? Add members' responses to the list. Responses should include prayer, Bible study, following the Spirit's leadership, worship, and Christian fellowship.

13. Say, A college student was having a difficult time keeping a pure mind. A friend accompanied him to his room to counsel with him about the problem. Every wall of the student's room had nude pictures from pornographic magazines. Ask, What was the first piece of advice the friend should have given the student?

14. Read Philippians 4:8 from several translations. List words or phrases that mean the same as the words in this verse, such as *pure* and *lovely*. Ask, What are we to do about things that are pure and lovely? (*Think on them.*)

15. Sum up the key to mind control by asking, Why is the Bible important in renewing your mind? (*It is God's revealed truth that has the power to change lives through mind renewal.*)

16. Discuss how meditation on memorized Scriptures renews our minds. Suggest that members listen to passages of recorded Scriptures. They may make their own recordings or purchase them.

17. Ask volunteers to share the commitments they made to get God's Word into their lives daily.

18. Emphasize that this study should not leave members with the impression that being God-centered, as opposed to being controlled by evil, makes us pawns. Each person determines to whom he or she will give control, and control is exercised only as the individual allows it to happen. Say, Yes, each person has a choice about the control that will be exercised over him or her. And that person is responsible and accountable to God for the choices he or she makes.

Take a stand-up break. Invite participants to help themselves to refreshments.

PART 2 (45/60 minutes)

Prayer Time (10 minutes)

1. Ask members to share specific prayer requests related to their week 2 assignment to do something kind for a member of their immediate or extended family who does not know Christ.

2. Briefly discuss "In the Carpenter's Shop." Ask a volunteer to share an area in which the Holy Spirit is helping him or her become more Christ-like and to put off old traits. Pray, thanking God for what was just shared as representative of what is occurring in the lives of members.

The Worldly Christian (10/15 minutes)

3. Invite members to find a partner, preferably not their spouse. Instruct each person to present to the other in his or her own words the Worldly Christian part of the Disciple's Personality. If they give most of the idea correctly, their partner should draw the horizontal line on the diamond in the "Minister to Others" segment of "My Walk with the Master This Week." Members are not expected to have learned the rest of the presentation. Remember that the Disciple's Personality is to be mastered a section at a time over a four-week period. Members can use any extra time to check on other assignments. If several members did not give most of the ideas correctly in this presentation, show the video presentation of the Disciple's Personality to refresh their memories.

"How to Listen to God's Word" (10/15 minutes)

4. Use James 1:22-25 as the key passage as you explain "How to Listen to God's Word" on pages 59-61 in the member book.

5. Ask members to use the questions based on the parable of the sower (Matt. 13:3-23) to determine what kind of hearers they usually are. Invite them to tell the group which classification they fall in.

6. Review the instructions based on James 1.

7. Ask members to look at the Hearing the Word form in the member book on page 141. Describe how to take notes on a sermon. Use the notes that you took this week as a model.

8. Encourage members to take notes on sermons and Sunday School lessons. Suggest that they begin a file of notes for future reference.

Testimony Outline (10/15 minutes)

9. Ask members to define and illustrate the word *testimony*. (Many television commercials use the testimony approach to sell products.)

10. Distinguish between the basic salvation testimony and other testimonies of the Christian life. Say, The testimony we will be working with during the rest of book 2 will be the salvation testimony. This testimony forms the foundation of all other Christian testimonies. Its length and use depend on the situation.

11. Ask members to turn to "Testimony Outline" on page 69 in the member book. Go over this material carefully and call attention to the assignment to write four facts about their conversions. Say, In week 4 you will build on this basic outline to develop your testimony further.

12. Give your personal testimony as a model for the members of the group. Be sure it is not longer than three or four minutes. After you have given your testimony, ask members to identify in it the points of the basic testimony outline.

13. Tell the group about the Testimony Workshop that will take place at the end of session 6. This will be a three-hour workshop. If you know the date for the workshop, announce it so members can put it on their calendars. If you have not set a date and the date is open for discussion, discuss with members various times, dates, and places. Encourage members to work on their testimonies between now and then. For many of them, this will be one of the most difficult assignments they do during this training. It will also be one of the most important.

14. Remind members that as part of this week's work, they are to share with a Christian friend the steps they've taken in beginning to outline their personal testimony.

Next Week's Assignments (5 minutes)

15. Ask members to look at "My Walk with the Master This Week" for week 3 on page 47 in the member book. Review the specific assignments. Distribute the large nails or sharp pencils. Call attention to the instructions in the member book for using them.

16. Address any problems or questions members may have. Praise them for their progress and encourage them to keep up the good work.

17. Announce the meeting time and place for next week. Close with prayer. Ask God to help each member place Christ first in their lives during the week ahead.

AFTER THE SESSION
❑ Evaluate the session by listing what you believe was effective. Consider ways to improve future sessions.
❑ Evaluate the response of individual members to the teaching on

renewing their minds. Talk with anyone you think needs personal help at this time.

❑ Look for opportunities to praise members sincerely, particularly any who may be experiencing problems. Offer your help as needed.

❑ Invite two members to visit or to minister with you during the week. Don't ask them to do anything they are not experienced in doing. The purpose is for them to observe. Before each visit, tell them what you expect to find and do. After the visit, talk about why you conducted the visit as you did. Use the Roman Road gospel presentation (book 1, pages 102-7) or the Gospel in Hand presentation (book 4, p. 128) when you witness each week so the members can become familiar with it before they are asked to learn it.

❑ Read "Before the Session" for Group Session 3. Evaluate the amount of preparation you will need for the next group session. At the top of the first page of session 3, record when you will prepare.

❑ Carefully study week 4 and do all the exercises in the member book. You will preview week 4 for members during session 3.

Split-Session Plan

FIRST WEEK

1. For the first week, follow part 1 of Group Session 2 as it is outlined in the Standard Plan, with the exception of the material on conversational prayer. That material will be used in the second week.

2. Lead the study "Renew Your Mind." Allow 20 minutes in your 45-minute session. Use the Standard Plan. Review items 7-12 only. Items 13-18 pertain to material members will study the second week.

3. Preview next week's assignments. Call attention to the fact that your group is using the Split-Session Plan. This means that members will verify only those assignments that pertain to the material they have studied that week. For example, members were assigned only days 1-3 for the first week of this session. Therefore, they would not be able to check off the assignment about conversational prayer because that assignment does not appear until day 5. The other assignments will be done the following week. Assign members days 4-5 in the study and adjourn the group.

SECOND WEEK

1. Divide the group in half (groups of four or five people). Ask members to share briefly about their week 2 assignment to do something kind for a member of their immediate or extended family who does not know Christ. Ask volunteers to share prayer requests related to that assignment. Suggest that members pray conversationally. Review the

material on conversational prayer. Invite members to pray and tell them you will pray last.

2. Pair members with persons other than their spouses. Each member of the pair should check the other person's "My Walk with the Master This Week." The boxes with the diagonal lines should be verified and marked. Romans 12:1-2 should be quoted accurately by each member before that assignment is marked.

3. Lead the study "Renew Your Mind." Spend a brief amount of time reviewing what members already have learned during the first week. Ask volunteers to summarize important points from last week's study. Then move to items 13-18.

4. Practice presenting the Worldly Christian part of the Disciple's Personality. Follow instructions in the Standard Plan for the presentation and for discussing the Worldly Christian.

5. Discuss "In the Carpenter's Shop." Follow instructions in the Standard Plan.

6. Preview next week's assignments. This period will not take as much time to explain because of the members' experience the previous week. Assign members days 1-3 in "Master Your Emotions." Members are to complete only assignments that pertain to those days. Close with prayer.

One-to-One Study Plan

Follow instructions in the Standard Plan. Make the following adjustments for the one-to-one relationship.

PART 1
1. Lead the study "Renew Your Mind." Be frank about the battle you have in keeping your mind on the right kind of thoughts. Ask where your one-to-one partner has problems. Share things you have found helpful in renewing your mind.

2. Share experiences you have had with conversational prayer. Ask the person to share experiences he or she had in praying conversationally with a family member, friend, or prayer partner this week. Pray conversationally with the person you are discipling.

PART 2
1. Present the material related to the Worldly Christian part of the Disciple's Personality and ask the person to note anything that is different

from the presentation in the member book. Ask the person to present the material on the Worldly Christian.

2. Preview next week's assignments. Explain "How to Listen to God's Word." Share with your partner experiences you have had in listening to sermons since you began using the Hearing the Word form and applying the principles.

GROUP SESSION 3
∽
Master Your Emotions

Session Goals

By the end of this session, members will be able to demonstrate their progress toward *MasterLife* goals by ...
- listing the four parts of a salvation testimony;
- completing week 3 assignments;
- explaining the Spiritual Christian part of the Disciple's Personality;
- praying for group members' requests regarding their testimonies or their sharing with a friend;
- describing how they benefitted from taking notes on a sermon;
- naming the six steps of the ACTION plan for mastering their emotions;
- applying the principles of mastering emotions to a case study;
- relating and applying previous weeks' studies to the Disciple's Personality.

Standard Plan

BEFORE THE SESSION
- ❑ Review week 3 and read and complete the learning activities for week 4 of *MasterLife 2: The Disciple's Personality.*
- ❑ Call members who are having problems completing assignments to ask them how they are doing this week and to encourage them.
- ❑ Master this week's material in the leader guide.
- ❑ Review the goals for this session.
- ❑ Check with the host or hostess to be sure he or she is ready for the group this week.
- ❑ Arrange the meeting place so that members can sit in a circle.
- ❑ Have pens or pencils and extra blank paper on hand for the session.
- ❑ Review in the member book "Guidelines for Writing Your Testimony" (p. 79). In part 2 of this session you will help members

prepare to gather materials for their testimonies during week 4 in order to write their testimonies before Group Session 5. Be prepared to encourage and affirm the work each member has done so far so they can take the next step toward writing their full testimonies.

❏ Contact the person you have enlisted to help you in the testimony-preparation time. Ask the person to be present during this week's session. Instructions for what this person is to do appear on page 96.

❏ If members have not kept up with their assignments using the Standard Plan or will not be able to give the Disciple's Personality successfully by week 4's group session, you may want to extend week 4 assignments over the next two weeks. To do this, use the Split-Session Plan for this session. Decide now so you can give the proper instructions for the plan you will use this week.

❏ Review the weekly studies to date and relate them to the Disciple's Personality.

❏ Have coffee or a soft drink with someone you do not like or with someone who does not like you. Be prepared to report on your experiences to the group.

DURING THE SESSION

PART 1 (45/60 minutes)

Introduction (25/30 minutes)
1. Begin the session on time even if all members are not present. During the presession time ask members to share their progress on overcoming problems in their work on their testimonies.

2. Begin with prayer. Ask members for reports on their experience in having coffee or a soft drink with someone they do not like or with a person who does not like them. Share your experience first; then invite others to share. Ask members to pray a sentence prayer for the person on his or her right pertaining to a request that person mentioned about sharing with a friend.

"My Walk with the Master This Week" (10 minutes)
3. Invite members to get with another person to quote Galatians 5:22-23 to each other. Make sure husbands and wives are not paired together. While members work in pairs, they can check each other's "My Walk with the Master This Week" and make the horizontal mark in the boxes after verifying work. Encourage members to share with their partners their strong and weak points in completing assignments.

Prayer Time (5 minutes)
4. Ask members to mention specific praises they have regarding their experiences in listening to a sermon this past week. Invite them to share

Testimony Outlines (20/30 minutes)

6. During the first half of this time period, arrange members in small groups of four. Review testimony outlines. Each person should "talk through" the basic facts of his or her testimony outlined during the work on "Testimony Outline." Ask members to be brief and factual. Members will not be sharing full testimonies at this point but are simply discussing the basic facts they have written down. Each person should be given about three minutes.

7. For the second half of this time period, work as a total group. Call attention to "Guidelines for Writing Your Testimony" on page 79 in the member book. Highlight suggestions that apply to problems that surfaced during the testimony-outline practice. Alert members to the following common errors of testimony writing so they can avoid them as they build their background information. Members will write their testimonies before Group Session 5.
- Not focusing on the salvation testimony. Other testimonies are appropriate for other people at other times, but the testimony they are writing is one to be shared with non-Christians.
- Reminiscing too much about things that would not be interesting to others.
- Sounding like a "holy Joe or Jane" who has all the answers.
- Too long.
- Either too specific about ages, places, and churches or so general that the testimony does not sound real.

8. Break members into groups of two to four people to talk through "Testimony Outline." Utilize the person you enlisted to help you by listening and making suggestions in the groups you are not in.

9. Remind members about the time and place for the Testimony Workshop at the end of session 6. Remind them that this will be a three-hour session. Invite questions about the workshop.

Next Week's Assignments (5 minutes)

10. Ask members to look at "My Walk with the Master This Week" for week 4 on page 72 and review the specific assignments. Make sure members understand how they are to complete each assignment.

11. Briefly preview the content of week 4. Ask members to complete the material "Present Your Body" before the next session.

12. Review the assignment about taking notes from a sermon as you continue to use the Hearing the Word form. Urge members to be on the alert for sermon references to the theme of presenting your body as a living sacrifice, the topic of week 4.

13. Call attention to the Who Are You? and Steps to Victorious Living parts of the Disciple's Personality they are to learn during next week's study. Explain that this material will help them recognize which portion of the Disciple's Personality describes them as they are today and will show steps they can take to be all Christ wants them to be.

14. Announce the time and place for the next meeting. Note the importance of 21 consecutive days of quiet times. Remind members that if they have not completed this assignment, they need to begin at the start of week 4 in order to have 21 consecutive days by the end of book 2.

15. Stand, join hands, and offer a prayer of dismissal. Ask each member to voice a one-sentence prayer for the person on his or her right. Say, Ask God to help this member grow in his or her relationship with Him through *MasterLife*.

AFTER THE SESSION

❑ Meet individually or in small groups with members who seemed to be having problems with the basic testimony outline.

❑ Encourage members who may be lagging behind in their assignments. Help them with any problems. If necessary, enlist another member to work with them.

❑ Take one or two members witnessing. You may want to visit some of the non-Christian persons whom they have listed on their Prayer-Covenant Lists. Model how to use your personal testimony.

❑ Pray for each member, using specific verses as the basis of your prayers. You may want to share with each person the verse you claimed for him or her. This could be done by card, telephone, or personal contact.

❑ Read "Before the Session" for Group Session 4 to evaluate the amount of time you will need to prepare for the next group session. Record at the top of the first page of the Group Session 4 material when you will prepare.

❑ Carefully study week 5 and do all the exercises in the member book. You will preview week 5 for members during session 4.

Split-Session Plan

FIRST WEEK

1. Divide the group in half (four to five people). Ask members to mention in their groups specific praises they have regarding their experiences in listening to a sermon this past week as they used the Hearing the Word form. Invite volunteers to pray short prayers of thanksgiving for the praise item just mentioned.

2. Ask members to report in their small groups on their experiences of having coffee with someone they do not like or with whom they feel estranged. Ask them to pray a sentence prayer for the person on their right pertaining to some request that person mentioned.

3. Ask members to work in pairs to check each other's assignments on "My Walk with the Master This Week."

4. Lead the study "Renew Your Mind." Review items 5 and 6 only. Items 7-9 pertain to material members will study next week.

5. Discuss "In the Carpenter's Shop." Follow instructions in the Standard Plan.

6. Preview next week's assignments. Assign members days 4-5 in the study. During this preview time, review only the assignments that they will be responsible for next week.

SECOND WEEK

1. Ask members to work in pairs to check off each other's "My Walk with the Master This Week." Instruct each person to draw the horizontal mark in the other member's diamond boxes after verifying work.

2. Instruct members to remain in pairs and present the Spiritual Christian section of the Disciple's Personality to each other.

3. Lead the study "Master Your Emotions." Spend about three minutes reviewing what members have already learned during the first week on this study. Ask volunteers to summarize important points from last week's study. Then move to items 7-9 in the Standard Plan.

4. Follow the Standard Plan for the "Testimony Outline" segment.

5. Preview next week's assignments. Follow the instructions in the Standard Plan. Assign members days 1-2 in "Present Your Body." Members are to complete only assignments that pertain to the material they study this week. Follow the Standard Plan for closure.

One-to-One Plan

PART 1

Along with the Standard Plan, help the person share particular emotions that he or she has difficulty mastering so that you can work with him or her in discovering Christ-honoring options. Be honest about the difficulties you have and share solutions that have worked for you.

PART 2

Give individual time to help this person share the story of his or her life with you so that you can recommend the best facts to use in a salvation testimony. Share any challenges you may have faced in learning to write your testimony.

GROUP SESSION 4

Present Your Body

Session Goals

By the end of this session, members will be able to demonstrate their progress toward *MasterLife* goals by …

- sharing ways they are becoming more Christlike in character;
- completing week 4 assignments;
- giving the entire presentation of the Disciple's Personality to another group member;
- applying to their lives the teaching of the study on the use of their bodies;
- praying about their victories and personal needs as well as those of others;
- sharing experiences of discussing with a friend their testimony preparation;
- preparing background material from which to write their testimonies before session 5;
- helping other members identify the key facts in preparing to write personal testimonies.

Standard Plan

BEFORE THE SESSION

❑ Review week 4 and read and complete the learning activities for week 5 of *MasterLife 2: The Disciple's Personality.*

❑ Pray daily for your group members. Some may become discouraged as the amount of work to accomplish before a session increases. Ask God for guidance and encouragement in each member's life.

❑ Master this week's material in the leader guide.

❑ Review the goals for this session.

❑ Check with the host or hostess to be sure he or she is ready for the group this week.

❑ Arrange the meeting place so that members can sit in a circle.

❑ Have pens or pencils, extra blank paper, and newsprint or a chalkboard on hand for activities.

❑ Review memory verses to date to be sure that you know them.

❑ Draw on newsprint or the chalkboard the basic picture of the Disciple's Personality as it appears in the member book (p. 90). Be sure to leave space to add the extra words between the circle and the words *God, Satan*. You will use this drawing in part 2 when you apply the Disciple's Personality using James 4:1-8. View the videotape if you need additional help with this presentation.

❑ Be prepared to share with members any additional information about the Testimony Workshop.

❑ Contact the person you have trained to be available to help you in the testimony evaluations during this session.

DURING THE SESSION

PART 1 (45/60 minutes)

Introduction (5 minutes)
1. Greet members as they arrive. Be alert and available to discuss any questions they may have. Begin on time with a prayer.

Testimony Evaluation (20/25 minutes)
2. Invite members to divide into two small groups. Lead one group while the other group members are led by the person you have trained.

3. Emphasize the necessity of focusing on the salvation testimony as they write their first drafts. Say, Testimonies of growth, tithing, prayer, and so on should be used at other times. You are preparing these testimonies for non-Christians.

4. Each person should list the items he or she added to the basic testimony outline during the work this past week. Members will not be sharing full testimonies at this point but are simply discussing the ways they have expanded the basic information and enhanced it from the previous week. Ask members to be brief and factual, with a limit of three minutes per testimony. Write down key words to help you remember points in each testimony. After members give their testimonies, encourage them to take notes as you give brief evaluations. Evaluate the testimony outlines using the following guidelines.
  • Comment on the things that are appropriate.
  • Note things that should be left out.
  • Ask questions to clarify vague areas.
  • Ask about other facts that should be included.
  • Ask other members to give their feedback about key facts in each others' testimonies.
  • Encourage members by expressing your faith in their ability to write the first draft next week.

5. Ask members to tell about their experiences discussing their testimonies with a friend. Ask them to share responses or suggestions made.

6. Close this part of the session by asking members to pray short prayers about the experiences they are having in working on their testimonies.

"My Walk with the Master This Week" (5 minutes)
7. Pair members with persons other than their spouses. Ask them to check each other's "My Walk with the Master This Week." Encourage members to use any extra time to review their memory verses.

"Present Your Body" (20/30 minutes)
8. Ask, How do you feel about your body? (Group response) Say, State one fact about your body that makes you glad. (Group response) Next, state one fact that makes you sad. (Group response) Now, state one fact that makes you mad. (Group response) A lively discussion should follow that will lead to a discussion of this week's study. Depending on members' responses, choose from items 10-12 the activities that relate to their needs. Do not exceed the time allowance.

9. Ask, What are the three functions the body performs in the world? Write them on newsprint or on the chalkboard. Ask for examples that members gave in the activity on page 74 about applying these three functions.

10. Say, Let's talk about the possibility of achieving those applications. What is working against you? *(flesh)* Who is working for you? *(Christ)* What three actions of Christ make it possible for your body to be used by God? *(incarnation, crucifixion, resurrection)*

11. Say, Sometimes it is difficult for you to know how to dedicate yourself to God; but if you present each member of your body to Him as a living sacrifice, it becomes clear. Ask volunteers to share their responses to the first exercise on page 87. Ask for volunteers to share the commitments they made on page 87-88 to honor Christ with their physical bodies.

12. Ask, Is the body good or evil? Say, In the history of the Christian faith two heresies about the body have arisen. According to both views, the body is presumed to be inherently evil. One group taught that the body was evil and had no relationship to the soul. Thus, people could do anything they wished with their bodies without affecting the spiritual condition. The other group believed that because the body is evil, it must be subdued constantly by beatings, self-denial, starvation, or other means of torture. Ask, What are the implications and consequences of each of these views? What are some contemporary examples?

13. Ask, Can the body sin without the soul being involved? Allow time for discussion. Use Matthew 12:34 and James 1:14-15 to stress the fact that such an idea is ridiculous. A person is a singular, undivided entity. Help members understand that terms such as *body, spirit,* and *soul* are used to reflect the different aspects of the total person. Say, If I sin, it is not my mind that has sinned; neither is it my body or my soul. It is I who have sinned and every part of who I am—body, mind, soul, and spirit—is involved.

14. Ask members to volunteer to give testimonies of how applying the incarnation, crucifixion, and resurrection to their daily lives makes it possible for their bodies to be instruments of righteousness. Pray, asking God to help members use their bodies for His glory and purposes.

Take a stand-up break. Invite participants to help themselves to refreshments.

PART 2 (45/60 minutes)

Prayer Time (5 minutes)
1. Call the group together for prayer. Ask volunteers to share a way they recognized during this week's study that they are experiencing victory every day with Christ.

2. Ask if anyone has an update on prayer requests that group members have mentioned during this study. Lead the group to pray short prayers related to the victories or the prayer requests mentioned.

The Disciple's Personality (20/25 minutes)
3. Ask members to work in pairs and present the Disciple's Personality to each other. If several members did not give most of the ideas correctly, you may want to give the entire presentation to the group or show the video presentation of the Disciple's Personality to refresh their memories. If one member of the pair did not have time to finish, suggest they find a time after the session or during the week to give it. If someone is not able to draw and explain the Disciple's Personality presentation, he or she will need to have you or another member privately meet with them and check his or her presentation before session 6.

4. Begin letting those who are ready to give the Disciple's Personality in its final form do so during this time period. As the leader, check off those who do it well. You will have time for only one or two members to present the Disciple's Personality in this session. In week 5 you'll have time to hear the remainder of the presentations.

"In the Carpenter's Shop" (5 minutes)

5. Ask a volunteer to share what is being removed from his or her life and what is being added as the Holy Spirit helps him or her become more Christlike in the area of presenting the body. Pray a prayer of thanksgiving for what this person has shared and for growth that others have experienced.

Training Session (10/15 minutes)

6. Show your basic drawing of the Disciple's Personality you made before the session.

7. Ask someone to read James 4:1-8. Invite three persons to listen for the *source* of our struggles in living the Christian life. Invite three others to listen for the *solution*. Mention that in this passage you will discuss what to do at each moment of temptation to gain victory.

8. Briefly discuss the reports from James 4:1-8 of the *source* of your struggles in the Christian life. *(Our lust and desires.)* Say, Look at James 4:5: "The Spirit Whom He has caused to dwell in us yearns over us—and He yearns for the Spirit [to be welcome]—with a jealous love" (AMP).[1] The Spirit is aggressively concerned about your victory.

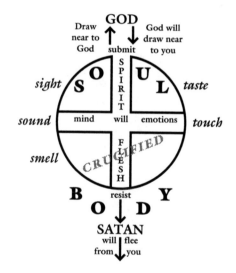

9. Discuss the actions Christians take to gain victory. Complete the drawing, using the following steps.
   - Add *submit* in the space above the word *Spirit*, with an arrow pointing up to *God*. Beside it write *Draw near to God*. Draw another arrow pointing down from God and beside it write *God will draw near to you.*
   - Write the word *resist* in the space below the word *flesh*, with an arrow pointing to *Satan*. Below the word *Satan* write the result *will flee from you* and another arrow pointing down from *Satan*.
   - Say, This is the correct order. If you resist Satan in your strength, you will fail. If you first submit to the Lord, you can resist Satan, and he will flee from you. If you send Christ to the door when Satan knocks, Satan will say, "Excuse me; I must have the wrong house." Study these principles in Romans 6, 8, and Galatians 3.

Next Week's Assignments (15 minutes)

10. Ask members to look at "My Walk with the Master This Week" for week 5 and review the specific assignments. Make sure they understand how to complete each assignment.

11. Briefly preview the content of week 5. Ask members to complete week 5, "Be Filled with the Spirit" before the next session.

12. Ask members to look at "Guidelines for Writing Your Testimony" on page 79 in the member book. Call attention to suggestions that

apply to challenges that surfaced during members' discussion of their testimony work. Explain that these guidelines will help them know if their testimony contains all appropriate elements. Instruct members to write a three-minute draft they can read to a small group during next week's session. This would be about 250-300 words or one typed, double-spaced page. Suggest that anyone who needs additional help with this assignment can view the videotape on testimonies.

13. Announce any additional information you may have about the Testimony Workshop. Invite questions about the workshop.

14. Call attention to the assignment about writing notes from a sermon on the Hearing the Word form. Say, Pay particular attention to applying the message to your life in the week ahead. Be on the alert for sermon references to the theme of being filled with the Spirit, our topic for next week.

15. Tell members that they will be asked to tell about ways they have used the Disciple's Personality presentation.

16. Remind members of the importance of having each item checked off on "My Walk with the Master" each week to keep these activities from accumulating at the end of the study. Offer individual help outside class if needed.

17. Announce the details for next week's meeting. Close with prayer.

AFTER THE SESSION

❏ Use the following questions to evaluate your group.
  • Do members care for one another? Are they trusting one another? Are they becoming more open with one another?
  • Are there blocks in communication?
  • Are spouses relating well as group members?
  • Are members responding well to my leadership?
  • Is the group becoming cliquish? Do I need to encourage members to keep reaching out?
  • Do some members show undesirable attitudes toward other members? Should I take them visiting together and/or pair them more often?
  • Are members helping disciple one another?
  • Do they see me as a growing disciple who is learning from them?
❏ Continue to invite members to go witnessing and ministering with you. Take them on church visitation or hospital calls.
❏ Call or see all members of the group this week to encourage, enable, or challenge them as needed. See if any need help completing assignments or working on their testimonies. Remember that you are their servant. Continue to look for opportunities to praise them.

❑ Pray for each member. Remember their prayer requests.
❑ Read "Before the Session" for Group Session 5 to evaluate the amount of time you will need to prepare for the next group session. At the beginning of session 5 material, record when you will prepare.
❑ Carefully study week 6 and do all the exercises in the member book. You will preview week 6 for members during session 5.

Split-Session Plan

FIRST WEEK

1. Follow the Standard Plan for working on testimonies, sharing their testimony with a friend, and checking each other's work in "My Walk with the Master This Week."

2. Lead week 4, "Present Your Body." Review items 10-12 only. Items 13-15 pertain to material members will study next week.

3. Preview next week's assignments. Assign members days 4 and 5 in the study. During this preview time, focus on the assignments they will be responsible for next week.

SECOND WEEK

1. Follow the Standard Plan for the remainder of the group session. Lead week 4, "Present Your Body." Spend about three minutes reviewing what members learned during the first week of the study. Ask volunteers to summarize important points from last week's study. Then move on to items 13-15.

2. Preview next week's assignments using the Standard Plan. Assign days 1-3 in week 5, "Be Filled with the Spirit." Members are to complete only assignments that pertain to the material they study this week.

One-to-One Plan

Follow instructions for the Standard Plan. In part 1 help your partner with any problems he or she has related to presenting the Disciple's Personality presentation. In part 2 help your partner organize background material to be used to write his or her testimony for next week's session. When you are presenting the application of the Disciple's Personality, read James 4:1-8 while the other person listens for the source and solution. Ask for a report as called for. View the videotape if you feel that would be helpful.

---

¹From *The Amplified New Testament* © The Lockman Foundation 1954, 1958, 1987. Used by permission.

GROUP SESSION 5

Be Filled with the Spirit

Session Goals

By the end of the session, members will be able to demonstrate their progress toward *MasterLife* goals by …
- completing week 5 assignments;
- answering questions related to the filling of the Spirit;
- using James 4:1-8 to apply the Disciple's Personality;
- applying a sermon to their lives;
- continuing the process of reading the first draft of their testimonies and receiving feedback;
- making plans for the Testimony Workshop;
- praying for persons in their and others' circles of influence.

Standard Plan

BEFORE THE SESSION

❑ Review week 5 and read and complete the learning activities for week 6 of the *MasterLife 2: The Disciple's Personality* member book.

❑ As you complete the study "Be Filled with the Spirit," prayerfully consider whether you are fully experiencing the Spirit.

❑ Pray daily for each member of your group. Some may become discouraged as the amount of work increases before a session. Ask God for guidance and encouragement in each member's life.

❑ Call each member and encourage him or her to attend.

❑ Master this week's material in the leader guide.

❑ Review the goals for this session.

❑ Check with the host or hostess to be sure he or she is ready for the group this week.

❑ Arrange the meeting place so that members can sit in a circle.

❑ Finalize plans for the Testimony Workshop. Be prepared to share plans with the group in this week's session. If the workshop is to be held away from the church, prepare a map of the location. Remind members that the workshop will be three hours long.

❑ Have pens or pencils and extra blank paper on hand for the session.

❑ Take notes on a sermon, using the Hearing the Word form on page 141. If you are a pastor, you may want to take notes on a taped sermon or on one preached over the radio or television. You will share with the group your notes on the application of the message. Be specific and open about what needs to be changed in your life.

❑ Draw again on newsprint or the chalkboard the basic picture of the Disciple's Personality. Leave room to add the extra words in the illustration. You will use this drawing when you apply the Disciple's Personality using Galatians 5:16-25. Use the videotape to help you prepare this portion of the session if needed.

❑ Review "How to Write Your Testimony" on pages 109-13 in the member book. Be prepared to critique members' outlines, using the criteria given in the article and the information in the following section of the leader guide.

❑ Preview the videotape on how to evaluate a testimony. This will help you evaluate testimonies and give feedback. It will also help you train the other person you enlisted to help you evaluate testimonies.

❑ Contact the person you have trained to help evaluate testimonies. Confirm that he or she will be present for this session.

DURING THE SESSION

PART 1 (45/60 minutes)

Introduction (20/25 minutes)
1. Begin with prayer. Ask for requests from group members.

2. Share your experience of taking notes on a sermon this week—including what you wrote in the personal-application section. Be honest about your shortcomings and what you have done or have not done to correct them. Then ask members who are willing to do so to share their notes on how they applied sermons they heard.

3. Ask one or two volunteers to report on the people for whom they prayed in their circles of influence this week. You may need to lead if others don't. Suggest that members not mention names but describe the types of situations in which they encounter these persons. Have a time of prayer in which volunteers pray for concerns that they have voiced about the people for whom they have prayed.

4. Pair members with persons other than their spouses to check each other's "My Walk with the Master This Week." Encourage them to use any extra time to review Scriptures they have memorized.

"Be Filled with the Spirit" (25/35 minutes)
Choose from the following items appropriate questions and activities for your group's study. Do not feel that you have to use each question. Do not exceed your time allowance.

5. Review the content by asking, How do people know they have the presence of the Holy Spirit within them? *(If they belong to Jesus.)* Then ask, How do they know if they have the power of the Holy Spirit? *(First by faith and then by the fruit and the gifts of the Spirit.)*

6. Call on a volunteer to read Ephesians 5:18. Ask, Which do you consider worse: being drunk with wine or not being filled with the Spirit? Invite discussion. Emphasize that we are all commanded to be filled; it is not an option for Christians. Point out that the apostles were accused of being drunk on the day of Pentecost. Ask, Why do you think observers thought the disciples were drunk? Allow time for discussion.

7. Ask volunteers to describe a time that they have tried to witness on their own strength. What was the result?

8. Review the list of the fruit of the Spirit in Galatians 5:22-23. Invite members to find synonyms for the nine nouns. Lead the group to describe a Spirit-filled person in terms of who that person is *(the fruit)* and what that person does *(gifts)*. Be sure members can relate these concepts to aspects of a person's lifestyle.

9. Ask members to read Ephesians 5:19-20 and identify two results of being filled by the Spirit. *(A Spirit-filled person is characterized by praising and thanking God.)*

10. Ask, What is the opposite of being filled with the Spirit? *(Being filled with self.)* Say, Relate your description of a Spirit-filled Christian to a non-Christian and a worldly Christian. Ask, How do they differ?

11. Select a volunteer to tell about the experience of doing the three things necessary to be filled with the Spirit. Ask the volunteer to express how he or she knows the filling occurred. *(By faith.)* Then ask, How often will you need to ask for this filling? *(Daily.)* Emphasize that being filled is not a once-in-a-lifetime experience like salvation. Ask someone who has experienced being filled with the Spirit in previous days to describe how this filling has affected his or her (1) personal character and (2) work for the Lord.

12. Close with sentence prayers of praise and thanksgiving for the fullness of the Spirit.

Take a stand-up break. Invite participants to help themselves to refreshments.

PART 2 (45/60 minutes)

Personal Testimonies (30/40 minutes)
1. Divide the members into two small groups. Lead one group while members in the other group review Scriptures they have memorized up to this point in the study.

2. Evaluate the first drafts of their testimonies. Instruct members to be brief and factual, with a limit of three minutes per testimony. Ask each person to read or give the first draft of his or her testimony while others listen.

3. Take notes on the testimony by writing key words or phrases separated by a diagonal slash mark. Put a plus or minus sign or a question mark above each of the words. The plus sign indicates strong material. The minus sign indicates material that should be omitted or improved. The question mark indicates that the member has more material that can be added or material that needs clarification. Your notes might appear as follows.

    +   -   +   ?

Good Home/Age 6/ Fear of Death/ Wreck/

  -         -

Lived 10 Places/ Convicted of Sin/

Using this note method, you can review the strong and weak parts of the testimony quickly and easily. Tell the member the strong parts first. Then tell him or her how to improve the other parts. Use the criteria given in "Guidelines for Writing Your Testimony" on page 79-81 in the member book. Keep your notes for the review of the revised version of the testimony next week. Encourage the person who has given the testimony to take notes as you give your brief evaluation. Ask the group to listen to other members' testimonies for ways to improve their own. Encourage members by expressing your faith in their ability to give their testimonies at the Testimony Workshop next week.

4. When you have finished evaluating the testimonies of one group, move to the other. While you are evaluating the testimonies in this group, ask those in the other group to check off each other's Disciple's Personality presentations. (You'll reverse this process in session 6. This provides an opportunity for everyone to give both presentations—the Disciple's Personality and the testimony—in the group.) If necessary, use the person you trained to evaluate testimonies if there is not enough time for you to get around to all members.

The Disciple's Personality (10 minutes)
5. Train members how to apply the Disciple's Personality, using Galatians 5:16-25. Show your drawing of the Disciple's Personality. Ask someone to read Galatians 5:16-25. Ask three persons to listen for actions Christians should take related to the Spirit. Ask three others to listen for actions Christians should take related to the flesh. Call for reports. Discuss the following actions related to the Spirit.
- led by the Spirit (v. 18)
- live by the Spirit (v. 25)
- walk in the Spirit (v. 25)
- fruit of the Spirit (v. 22)

6. Ask members to tell ways they have used the Disciple's Personality presentation.

Next Week's Assignments (5/10 minutes)

7. Ask members to look at "My Walk with the Master This Week" for week 6 and preview the assignments for this session. Make sure members understand how to complete each assignment. Highlight that few new assignments are given to allow time for them to complete all assignments by the next session. Remind members that they will need to have all assignments in their "My Walk with the Master This Week" sections completed by the Testimony Workshop.

8. Briefly preview the content of week 6. Ask members to complete week 6, "Live Victoriously."

9. Instruct members to rewrite the first drafts of their testimonies for the Testimony Workshop, incorporating the suggestions given them during the critique. They may also want to summarize them on a three-by-five-inch card.

10. At the Testimony Workshop members should be prepared to give their testimonies in three minutes. They will give the testimony several times—once to you and then to persons role-playing a seeker, a self-satisfied person, and a skeptic. Relieve any fears by telling members that those playing the roles will be passive and will not make it difficult for them. Members will be able to use their notes on the card if necessary.

11. Call attention to the assignment about writing notes from a Sunday School lesson or a sermon. Urge members to particularly be on the alert for references to the theme of living victoriously, the topic of week 6.

12. Review final details of the Testimony Workshop. Distribute maps, if necessary. Invite questions. Announce plans for transportation to the site, if the workshop is held away from your regular meeting area. Ask for volunteers to provide rides for others, if needed.

13. Close with prayer. Thank God for the progress members have made. Ask for courage, wisdom, and efficient use of time in the week ahead to prepare for the remaining sessions. Pray that each member will be filled with the Spirit continually.

AFTER THE SESSION

❏ Immediately after the session, meet individually or in small groups with those who did not have notes on their personal testimonies critiqued or who had special problems.

- Suggest why they had difficulty.
- Show them how to overcome their difficulties.
- Get them started writing part of it.
- Keep them working by checking back or by assigning another person to help them during the week.

❑ Send a written announcement about the Testimony Workshop and encouraging each person to be present. Everyone should attend this workshop. Use the sample invitation below.

> *In acknowledgment of your walk with the Master*
> *during the past six weeks and to celebrate your completion of*
> MasterLife 2: The Disciple's Personality,
> *you are cordially invited to attend a*
> *Testimony Workshop.*
> *(time • date • place)*
>
> *Please bring your book indicating your completed assignments and*
> *the final draft of your testimony.*

❑ If the retreat is held away from the meeting site, furnish a phone number where members can be reached. Furnish other instructions if members are to bring a sack lunch or other items.

❑ Pray for members as they prepare to present their testimonies.

❑ Take two members with you to minister or to witness. By now you should have taken everyone in the group with you at least once. Perhaps you can visit some of the persons on their prayer lists.

❑ Contact the meeting site for the Testimony Workshop to confirm arrangements for food, lodging, meeting space, and other matters. Arrange for any materials you need for the workshop.

❑ Read "Before the Session" for week 6 to evaluate the amount of time you will need to prepare for your next group session. At the top of the week 6 material record when you will prepare.

❑ Begin to preview *MasterLife 3: The Disciple's Victory*. You will preview book 3 for members during the Testimony Workshop.

Split-Session Plan

FIRST WEEK

1. Follow the Standard Plan for the introduction to include checking each other's work in "My Walk with the Master This Week."

2. Lead week 5, "Filled with the Spirit." Review items 5-7 only. Items 8-12 pertain to materials members will study next week.

3. Preview next week's assignments. Assign members days 4-5 in the study. During this time, review only the assignments they will be responsible for next week.

SECOND WEEK

1. Follow the Standard Plan for part 2. Lead the study "Be Filled with the Spirit." Spend about three minutes reviewing what members learned during the first week. Ask volunteers to summarize important points from last week's study. Then move on to items 8-12.

2. Preview next week's assignments. Assign members days 1-3 in week 6, "Live Victoriously," and all assignments pertaining to the material in days 1-3.

One-to-One Plan

Follow instructions for the Standard Plan. In part 2 spend time helping the person finalize his or her testimony. Discuss other possible testimonies in addition to the salvation testimony. Discuss when and how a personal testimony may be used. Repeat your testimony as a model. When you are presenting the application of the Disciple's Personality, read Galatians 5:16-25 while the other person underlines the actions related to the flesh and to the Spirit.

GROUP SESSION 6

Live Victoriously

Session Goals

By the end of this session, members will be able to demonstrate their progress toward *MasterLife* goals by ...
- completing week 6 assignments;
- finalizing plans for the Testimony Workshop;
- sharing successes and failures in living the victorious life;
- sharing ways they have used the Disciple's Personality in their everyday lives;
- sharing ways they have seen other members changed by *MasterLife 2: The Disciple's Personality;*
- continuing to read the first drafts of their testimonies and having them critiqued.

Standard Plan

BEFORE THE SESSION

❑ Review week 6 and read the activities for the Testimony Workshop.

❑ As you complete week 6, "Be Filled with the Spirit," prayerfully consider whether you are living a victorious life in the Spirit.

❑ Pray daily for each member of the *MasterLife* group. Ask God for guidance and encouragement in each member's life.

❑ Call each member of the group to confirm attendance at the final group session and the Testimony Workshop.

❑ Master this week's material in the leader guide.

❑ Review the goals for this session.

❑ Check with the host or hostess to be sure he or she is ready for the group this week.

❑ Arrange the meeting place so that members can sit in a circle.

❑ Make any last-minute plans for the Testimony Workshop. You will want to share them with group members in this week's session. The next time you meet after session 6 will be for the Testimony Workshop. The workshop will be three hours in length. Provide an emergency number where members can be reached if necessary.

❑ Have pens or pencils and extra blank paper on hand for the session.

❑ Contact the person you have asked to help you evaluate testimonies. Ask this person to be present during session 6.

DURING THE SESSION

PART 1 (45/60 minutes)

Introduction (10/15 minutes)
1. Greet members and express appreciation for their participation in the group. Begin with prayer.

2. Say, Share one change you have seen in the life of the person seated to your right since the beginning of *MasterLife 2: The Disciple's Personality.* Go around the circle until each member has answered.

3. Ask each person to pray and thank God in a sentence or two for the progress in *MasterLife* that the person to his or her left has mentioned about himself or herself.

Verifying Assignments (10 minutes)
4. Pair members with persons other than their spouses to check "My Walk with the Master This Week." Encourage them to use extra time to review Scriptures memorized. All members are to have all assignments checked off by the end of the upcoming Testimony Workshop.

The Disciple's Personality (5/10 minutes)

5. Ask members to share experiences when they used the Disciple's Personality during the past week.

6. Ask two volunteers to share how they applied Galatians 5:16-25 to their lives this past week.

"Live Victoriously" (20/25 minutes)

Choose from the following items appropriate questions and activities for your group's study. Do not feel that you have to use each question. Do not exceed your time allowance.

7. Explain in your own words how the Disciple's Personality explains the possibility of defeat or victory in the life of a disciple.

8. Divide members into two small groups or enlist two volunteers to discuss the following questions.
   Group 1: In what ways does Satan influence human personality?
   Group 2: In what ways does the world influence human personality for good? for bad?

9. Ask the group to summarize how Jesus' death and resurrection bring victory over sin. Then ask, How important to a victorious Christian life is your crucifixion with Christ? *(Death to the old person makes possible the new life.)*

10. Ask a group member to quote Galatians 2:20. Choose a volunteer to recall the two dynamics of victory this verse mentions. *(Death and life.)* Ask, What motivated Jesus' action on your behalf? *(He loved you and gave Himself for you.)*

11. Lead a Scripture search of Romans 6:11-13 to discover three commands that keep you from a lifestyle of sin. *(Think of yourself as dead to sin; don't let sin have control; don't offer any part of your body to sin.)* Ask, Which of these commands do Christians violate most often?

12. Encourage members to memorize 1 Corinthians 10:13. Discuss the difference between temptation and sin. *(Jesus was tempted but did not sin. Sin is yielding to temptation.)* Ask, Where does temptation stop and sin begin? Offer the following analogy: You cannot stop the birds from flying over your head, but you can keep them from building a nest in your hair!

13. Point out that when a fleeting, wrong thought becomes a subject that you dwell on and when you let your mind entertain the idea, you have sinned regardless of whether you have acted on the impulse. Read Jesus' example in Matthew 5:27-28. Suggest that the following mental

discipline is one way of dealing with temptation. Say, As you are experiencing temptation, picture a cross. Think of Jesus dying on the cross for the very sin you are contemplating. Remember His victory over that particular sin. Thank Jesus for His victory and for your victory. Ask volunteers to share victories they have experienced recently. Call for testimonies of how persons have been able to overcome habits that kept them bound by sin.

14. Review the seven steps to Christlike character on page 139. Make sure members understand the implications of each step. Ask group members to pray silently, thanking God for His forgiveness and cleansing. Then lead a spoken prayer, praising God for Jesus' victory over sin.

Take a stand-up break. Invite participants to help themselves to refreshments.

PART 2 (45/60 minutes)

Personal Testimonies (40/50 minutes)
1. Continue the process you began last week of evaluating personal testimonies. Keep the same divisions you used last week. Lead the group that you did not get to work with while members in the other group check each other's Disciple's Personality presentations. Use the person you trained to evaluate testimonies if there is not enough time for you to get around to all members. As members listen to other members' testimonies, encourage them to make mental notes of ways to improve their own. Encourage members by expressing your faith in their ability to give their testimonies at the Testimony Workshop next week.

Next Week's Assignments (5/10 minutes)
2. Remind members that they will need to have all assignments in their "My Walk with the Master This Week" sections completed by the Testimony Workshop next week.

3. Instruct members to rewrite the first drafts of their testimonies, incorporating suggestions given during the critique. Remind them that they can summarize on one three-by-five-inch card. Members should be prepared to give their testimonies in three minutes. They will give the testimony several times—to you and then to persons who will be role-playing a seeker, a self-satisfied person, and a skeptic. Relieve any fears by telling members that those playing the roles will not make it difficult for them. Members will be able to use their notes on the card if necessary.

4. Review final details for the Testimony Workshop. Invite questions. Explain transportation arrangements to the site if the workshop is held away from your regular meeting area. Distribute the telephone number where members can be reached.

5. Close with prayer. Thank God for what members have learned about themselves in preparing their personal testimonies. Ask for courage, wisdom, and efficient use of time in the week ahead to prepare for the Testimony Workshop. Pray that each member will be filled with the Spirit continually.

AFTER THE SESSION

❑ Meet individually or in small groups with those who did not have notes on their personal testimonies critiqued or who had problems.
  • Suggest why they had difficulty.
  • Show them how to overcome their difficulties.
  • Get them started writing part of it.
  • Keep them working by checking back or by assigning another person to help them during the week.
❑ Make any final arrangements needed for the Testimony Workshop.
❑ Read "Before the Session" for the Testimony Workshop to evaluate the amount of time you will need to prepare. At the top of the Testimony Workshop material record when you will prepare.
❑ Finish previewing *MasterLife 3: The Disciple's Victory*. You will preview book 3 for members during the Testimony Workshop.

Split-Session Plan

FIRST WEEK
1. Follow the Standard Plan for part 1. Use only items 7-9 in "Live Victoriously." The remaining items pertain to next week's material.

2. Preview next week's assignments. Assign members days 4-5 in the study. Preview only assignments they will be responsible for next week.

SECOND WEEK
1. Follow the Standard Plan for part 2. Lead the study "Live Victoriously." Spend about three minutes reviewing what members learned during the first week of the study. Ask volunteers to summarize important points from last week's study. Then move on to items 10-14.

2. Preview next week's assignments using the Standard Plan. The next session is the Testimony Workshop. The workshop is not a split-session.

One-to-One Plan

Follow instructions for the Standard Plan. Spend extra time helping the other person finalize his or her testimony if needed.

Testimony Workshop

Note to those using the Split-Session Plan and the One-to-One Plan: The *split-session plan* is not appropriate for the Testimony Workshop. The workshop should be scheduled at a time when three uninterrupted hours can be devoted to it. The Testimony Workshop does not work as well with the *one-to-one plan* unless several pairs would like to do the training simultaneously. However, you can follow the same step-by-step plan and either find someone to role-play the different persons or play each of the roles yourself. The goal is the same—that the person will be able to master his or her testimony and give it to different types of persons in a role-play situation before giving it in real life. If the person has already been giving the testimony, this session will allow him or her to clarify and sharpen it. As a follow-up, arrange for the person to give his or her testimony in a small group or in a witnessing situation.

Workshop Goals

By the end of this three-hour workshop, members will be able to demonstrate their progress toward *MasterLife* goals by …

- sharing testimonies of growth in Christ during *MasterLife 2: The Disciple's Personality;*
- completing all assignments in *MasterLife 2: The Disciple's Personality;*
- revising their personal salvation testimonies to meet the stated criteria;
- adjusting their salvation testimonies to fit the needs of persons playing the roles of a seeker, a self-satisfied person, and/or a skeptic;
- examining ways they plan to seek continued growth in Christ.

BEFORE THE WORKSHOP

❑ Be prepared to give members an overview of the basic content of the next book, *MasterLife 3: The Disciple's Victory.*

❑ Call each member of the group and encourage him or her to attend. Make sure all members understand that they are to bring to this meeting the salvation testimony they have written.

❑ Master workshop material in this leader guide.

❑ Review the goals for the Testimony Workshop.

❑ Check on arrangements for the Testimony Workshop. Check the meeting site to be sure it is ready for the group.

❑ Make plans for starting the study of *MasterLife 3: The Disciple's Victory.* Arrange a time, date, and place for the first meeting. Be prepared to share these plans with group members. Have books on hand at the workshop for members to purchase.

❑ Choose either to show the video presentation of the Spiritual Armor or to make the presentation yourself. If you choose to present the material yourself, preview the way Avery Willis does it on the videotape. Then develop your own script. If you choose to show the video, secure video equipment and cue the tape before the session begins.

❑ Have pens or pencils and extra blank paper on hand for the workshop.

❑ Contact the person you have trained to colead. Make sure this person knows about workshop arrangements (time, date, place) and what his or her responsibilities are.

❑ Prepare to evaluate each testimony. Review the procedures. Approach your task prayerfully. Scores of potential decisions for Christ may result from this equipping ministry. The attitude you take as you perform this task is important. You are a servant, not a critic. Avoid making group members feel they are being tested and can either pass or fail. Lead them to rely on the work of the Holy Spirit as they write and give their testimonies.

❑ Pray for the workshop. Members need to have a sense of accomplishment and success at the end of *MasterLife 2: The Disciple's Personality*. They will get this from having all their work in "My Walk with the Master This Week" checked off and by successfully completing their written testimonies.

❑ Enlist three people in your church who will agree to play the roles of unbelievers in the Testimony Workshop. Explain the purpose of the workshop and give them the following instructions.

1. Each of you will play one of the roles of an unbeliever: a skeptic, a seeker, or a self-satisfied person. As you role-play, you will wear a three-inch-by-five-inch card with your role name written on the card.

2. Assume the mental state of the particular unbeliever assigned to you. Act out how such a person thinks and speaks.

3. I will make an assignment, or you can choose a role you feel comfortable playing.

4. As you role-play …

    a. Be sincere in the role you play. Respond realistically. It is as insincere to *underplay* as to *overplay* the role.

    b. Don't throw any curves at the group members. They need positive reinforcement, not discouragement.

    c. Be open in order to draw the members into sharing the testimony.

    d. Spend 3 to 5 minutes with each person and no more than 10 minutes with each team. Expect each person to share his or her testimony; respond separately to each.

    e. Avoid critiquing the testimony. Simply play the role.

    f. Use concluding comments to reflect your position as an unbeliever but not to reject either the person or the testimony.

Before the session, practice with the role players by playing the part of a group member. Present your own testimony to the skeptic; then, let the others assist you in evaluating the way that role player responded. Repeat the procedure with seeker and self-satisfied. This practice will help the role players feel confident when they meet the group.

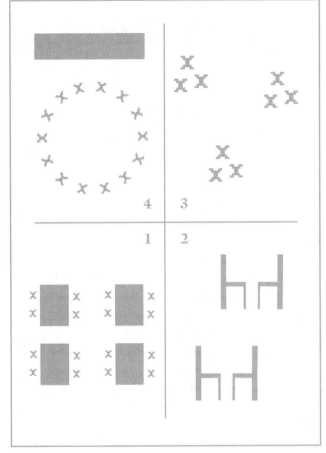

❑ Prepare the meeting room. Divide a large room into four areas, or use four available rooms for the functions shown in the drawing above. In the first area provide tables, paper, and pencils for members as they work on their drafts. In the second area, provide spaces for you and your coleader to meet with each person to evaluate testimonies. In the third area provide three sets of three chairs. In this section the role players will meet with the teams. In the fourth area provide light refreshments and provide a circle of chairs where members sit for activities not included in the actual testimony time.

❑ Prepare the following as a printed agenda to be distributed or write it on a poster or chalkboard.

Today's Workshop Agenda
- Have your testimony evaluated.
- Revise it as needed.
- Share it with role players.
- Make adjustments as needed.
- Share final version and/or discuss it with the workshop leader.

DURING THE WORKSHOP

PART 1 (3 hours)

Icebreaker (5 minutes)

1. Greet members as they arrive. Begin on time. Ask members to share the changes they have seen in themselves during this study of *MasterLife 2: The Disciple's Personality.*

2. Pray together. Ask each person to thank God in a sentence or two for the progress group members have made in *MasterLife.*

Verifying Assignments (10 minutes)

3. Ask members to pair up and check assignments for book 2. If a member needs a few extra minutes to complete an assignment, arrange to meet with that person during a break in the workshop.

General Instructions (15 minutes)

4. Introduce your assistant for the workshop. Point out that throughout the workshop members should go back to the same leader with whom they start.

5. Introduce the three guest "unbelievers" by their roles (skeptic, seeker, self-satisfied), not by name.

6. Tell members that you will be using "Guidelines for Writing Your Testimony" (member book, pp. 79-81) to evaluate their testimonies.

7. Ask each person to select a partner for the workshop. If this will be a problem, you can appoint them.

8. Call attention to the refreshment area. Suggest that a good time to get refreshments would be when partners are at the work area discussing the experiences they had with one of the role players.

Testimony-Sharing Time (2 hours)

9. Explain the procedure, using the written agenda you prepared.

- Say, You and your partner will move at your own pace. You are free to change the order of events if a workshop leader or role player is occupied. Use extra time to practice sharing testimonies, complete or review assignments, or recite Scripture you have memorized.
- Say, Half of the teams will have their written testimonies evaluated by one workshop leader, and the other teams will have theirs evaluated by the other leader. After reading them, the leader will make suggestions for improvements.
- Say, After the testimonies have been evaluated, you and your partner should go to the work area to make adjustments in your testimonies you think are necessary. You may want to make notes on a three-by-five-inch card to use when you give your testimony to the role players.
- Say, When you have adjusted written drafts, go to one of the three role players. Partners take turns; one witnesses while the other observes. Each partner opens the conversation with the role player, shares his or her testimony, and concludes with a leading question.
- Say, After both of you have witnessed to the role player, return to the work area to evaluate the experience. Discuss difficulties you had and make suggestions to each other. Discuss other facts in "Testimony Outline" (p. 69) that could be used with that type person. Make adjustments necessary to your testimony. Repeat the process with the other role players.
- Say, Finally, you and your partner should share your testimonies verbally with the workshop leader who read your testimonies earlier. Do not use notes unless necessary. Ask any questions that have arisen in the workshop.

10. This item covers instructions for leaders. Review each person's first draft, asking and answering questions, and making suggestions. Spend approximately 5 to 10 minutes with each person. Let the partner listen so he or she can support the other person. Concentrate on the following areas.

- Look for the story line. Avoid tampering with it, for it tells how Christ entered a person's life. However, if the story line is not present or if it is unclear, the testimony will not sound authentic. In these cases, suggest that it be strengthened in the next draft.
- Examine all parts of the testimony. Are they equally developed? If not, recommend that

attention be given to weak areas. If a person is using the thematic approach, the first part does not have to be well developed.

- Check to see that the four doctrinal truths are well expressed in part 3. Make suggestions to strengthen this area.
- Evaluate the amount of detail in the testimony. If it leaves out too many details, suggest other facts be added; if it includes unnecessary details, ask that they be summarized or deleted.
- Be sure the final sentence leads to further conversation.
- Search for church words and religious jargon. The testimony should not sound preachy.

Be available to counsel persons when you are not evaluating testimonies. It is not uncommon during the workshop to have someone receive his or her assurance of salvation or make a decision for Christ.

11. Give a signal when 1 hour is left and again when 30 minutes are left in this period. The latter signal alerts members to share their testimonies with one of the workshop leaders even if they have not shared it with all role players. Stop on time unless agreement is reached by all on extending the session. Another option is to plan a follow-up session.

12. Call the group back together. Thank the role players and give them permission to leave.

PART 2 (45 minutes)

The Spiritual Armor

1. Preview *MasterLife 3: The Disciple's Victory* by sharing study titles and giving a brief content overview.

2. Show the video segment or give the Spiritual Armor presentation yourself (member book, p. 129).

3. Ask for volunteers to give personal testimonies of what the group and *MasterLife* have meant to them. To get this time started, share your feelings.

4. Distribute copies of *MasterLife 3: The Disciple's Victory*. Assume all group members will continue in *MasterLife* unless they tell you otherwise. Encour-

age those members who may be considering not continuing. Assure group members that regardless of their decision, you will always be available to talk or pray with them and help them with their life in Christ.

5. Pray for group members. Say, As I pray, commit to God your decision about continuing in *MasterLife*. Ask God to speak to you about His will for you.

6. Ask the group if they would like to take a couple of weeks off or begin the next study immediately. Sound a note of victory and excitement about the next study theme.

7. Announce the time, date, and place of the beginning of the next study. Close with a prayer of thanksgiving and celebration.

AFTER THE WORKSHOP

- ❏ Write members expressing appreciation for their participation in the course.
- ❏ Finalize plans for beginning *MasterLife 3: The Disciple's Victory*. Confirm the time and meeting site. Post a notice on a church bulletin board and in publications to announce the formation of the group. Occasionally, someone who completed book 2 earlier than your group did will want to join your group. Welcome their involvement but be careful not to exceed the maximum capacity for a *MasterLife* group.
- ❏ If you question whether a group member will move on to the next book, call and encourage his or her participation. If a member informs you that he or she is unable to participate now, suggest that the person may want to join another group later.
- ❏ This is a good time to take stock of the leadership you are providing. If you believe that a problem exists between you and one of the members, visit with this person and clear the air.
- ❏ Spend time in prayer for each member.
- ❏ Inform the church of the progress of the group. Ask the church staff when and where some of your members can share testimonies about what *MasterLife* has meant to them. This is also a good time to enlist members to begin new *MasterLife* groups.

THE DISCIPLE'S VICTORY

MasterLife

BOOK 3

You, dear children, are from God and have overcome them, because the one who is in you is greater than the one who is in the world (1 John 4:4).

God will use *The Disciple's Victory* to lead group members to experience victories over the world, the flesh, and the devil in spiritual warfare.

❏ If members have not studied *MasterLife 1: The Disciple's Cross* and *MasterLife 2: The Disciple's Personality* or a significant amount of time has elapsed between studies, either schedule a separate session to overview this material, invite them to stay after this session, ask a person in the group to explain it later, or provide the videotapes of the presentations for them to take home. Provide a chalkboard or poster paper to draw the Disciple's Cross and the Disciple's Personality. Draw the cross and the personality as you give the presentations. Consider showing the video that accompanies the study.

❏ If members of your group were not part of the same group that studied *MasterLife 2: The Disciple's Personality*, and are not acquainted, have material for name tags for everyone you expect to attend.

❏ Have pens or pencils and extra blank paper on hand for the session.

❏ Choose either to show the video presentation of the Spiritual Armor or to make the presentation yourself. If you choose to present the material yourself, preview the way Avery Willis does it on the videotape. Then develop your own script. If you choose to show the video, secure video equipment and cue the tape before the session.

❏ Consider other uses of the video presentation of the Spiritual Armor.
  • Loan the tape to any member who missed the presentation or who would like to see it again for personal follow-up.
  • Encourage members to watch it again as they practice drawing their own graphics.
  • Show it during the Prayer Workshop.
  • Show it to new Christians as part of their initial discipleship.
  • Loan the presentation to someone you are counseling. They may identify reasons for negative emotions and bad thoughts. In this situation draw the diagrams yourself and use the principles discussed in the presentation as you share with the person.

❏ Plan to stay within the times given for each activity. The maximum time suggested for each week is 45 to 60 minutes for each part. Because it is an introduction, times for this week's session are 35 to 50 minutes for each part. You may want to print an agenda each week with the subjects and times listed. This will guide the group and allow members to help the group stay on schedule.

❏ Prepare to show your prayer journal as an example of what members' prayer journals will look like at the end of the study.

❏ Be prepared to tell members about the Prayer Workshop to be held at the conclusion of the study.

Remember that allowing members to share freely is far more important than sticking legalistically to a schedule. Group members sometimes arrive at a session eager to tell about something that happened in their lives during the week related to that week's content. Be sensitive to this need, and be flexible. Allow God to work in your group. Provide opportunities for everyone to respond during the session.

DURING THE SESSION

PART 1 *(35/50 minutes)*

Introduction (10 minutes)

1. Welcome each person and point members to the refreshments. If members were not together for the study of *MasterLife 2: The Disciple's Personality*, invite each person to make a name tag. As members arrive, introduce each person to the others in the room if they don't know each other. Let everyone visit informally until time to begin.

2. Begin promptly. Remind the group that you will begin and end each session on time. If group members want to fellowship or have additional discussions after the sessions, they may do so, but they can count on you to be prompt.

3. Ask each person to share one fact about himself or herself that group members may not know. Even if members of this group were together in *MasterLife 2: The Disciple's Personality*, they still may not know some facts about members' lives. Lead in prayer thanking God for guiding group members to participate in *MasterLife 3: The Disciple's Victory*.

Overview of *The Disciple's Victory* (5/10 minutes)

4. If this group did not participate in *MasterLife 2: The Disciple's Personality* and therefore did not attend the Testimony Workshop or if considerable time has elapsed between the conclusion of the workshop and the start of this course, you may want to spend more time on the overview and course goals. Preview by reviewing the weekly titles and giving a brief overview of the content of *MasterLife 3: The Disciple's Victory*. Distribute copies of the book to group members.

The Disciple's Cross (10/15 minutes)

5. If this group did not participate in *MasterLife 1: The Disciple's Cross*, you will need to briefly overview the Disciple's Cross presentation. Refer to the Disciple's Cross drawing in *MasterLife 3: The Disciple's Victory* (member book, p. 126) and to the full presentation in *MasterLife 1: The Disciple's Cross*.

6. Draw the Disciple's Cross on the chalkboard or on newsprint/poster paper as a point of reference. Say, You will have assignments in each of the six disciplines each week: spending time with the Master, living in the Word, praying in faith, fellowshipping with believers, witnessing to the world, and ministering to others.

7. Explain how the Disciple's Cross ties in with the Disciple's Personality, which you will highlight next. Say, The circle in the center of the Disciple's Cross represents you—your total personality, a unity.

Understanding what the circle represents helps you understand why you act the way you do.

8. Invite members who are not familiar with the Disciple's Cross to stay after the session for a full presentation, or ask a person in the group who was part of *MasterLife 1: The Disciple's Cross* to give the presentation after this session. Or loan them the videotape that features the presentation of the Disciple's Cross.

The Disciple's Personality (10/15 minutes)
9. If the group did not participate in *MasterLife 2: The Disciple's Personality*, briefly mention the Disciple's Personality presentation. Refer to the Disciple's Personality drawings in *MasterLife 3: The Disciple's Victory* (member book, p. 127-8) and to the full presentation in *MasterLife 2: The Disciple's Personality*.

10. Draw the Disciple's Personality on the chalkboard or on newsprint/poster paper as a point of reference. Do not explain it in detail as you draw.

11. Explain how the Disciple's Personality ties in with the Spiritual Armor, which is the focus of *MasterLife 3: The Disciple's Victory*. Say, The Disciple's Personality presentation prepares you for the war against the world, the flesh, and the devil as you understand how the Holy Spirit works in you to build Christlike character and helps give you inner victory. This inner victory prepares you for the outer victory you will learn how to attain in *MasterLife 3: The Disciple's Victory*. You will learn the defensive weapons of the Spiritual Armor, which protect you, and the offensive weapons, which lead you forward.

12. Invite members not familiar with the Disciple's Personality to stay after the session for you to give the full presentation, or ask a person in the group who was part of *MasterLife 2: The Disciple's Personality* to give the presentation after this session. Or loan them the videotape that features the presentation of the Disciple's Personality.

Take a stand-up break. Invite participants to help themselves to refreshments.

PART 2 (45/60 minutes)

Prayer Time (5 minutes)
1. Ask each member to pair with another person, preferably not his or her spouse. Invite members to share with the other person a concern they have in their lives. Instruct them to pray for each other's needs.

The Spiritual Armor (15/20 minutes)

2. Say, The Spiritual Armor expands on Prayer and the Word of God, the vertical bar of the Disciple's Cross that keeps us abiding in Christ. We want to expand on the inner victory that we learned to have in *MasterLife 2: The Disciple's Personality* with the outer victory that we can have when we use the spiritual weapons Christ has given us.

3. Give or view the Spiritual Armor presentation on pages 129-31 in the member book. Give it as a personal testimony of how you put on the Spiritual Armor in prayer. Say, The Spiritual Armor is to be mastered a section at a time over the next six weeks. Eventually, you will give the presentation in the correct order. However, the weekly study of each part does not follow the order in the Spiritual Armor presentation but follows the emphasis of the week.

Week 1 Assignments (10/20 minutes)

4. Ask members to look at "My Walk with the Master This Week" on page 8 for week 1 of *MasterLife 3: The Disciple's Victory* and review the specific assignments. Say, It will be important for you to complete each discipleship activity because it will provide an opportunity to learn by experience. A part of *MasterLife* is an accountability process through which we check each other's learning. When you complete an assignment, you will draw a vertical line through the diamond located in front of the assignment. A fellow member verifying your work during the group session will draw a horizontal line through the diamond to form a cross.

5. Preview the content of week 1. Ask members to complete the activities in the material "Overcoming the Enemy" before session 1 of *MasterLife 3: The Disciple's Victory*.

6. Encourage members to use the prayer guides that appear in each week of *MasterLife 3: The Disciple's Victory*. "Guide to Thanksgiving" on page 13 of the member book is an example. Urge them to begin using the guide during their prayer time the first week. Explain that they will include these guides in the prayer journals they will prepare later in the study. Show them your prayer journal as an example.

7. Call attention to the assignment involving the Relational-Witnessing Chart. Say, The circle at the center of the chart on page 135 may remind you of the center of the Disciple's Cross and the picture of the Disciple's Personality. A circle in *MasterLife* presentations always represents the disciple. Christ wants to flow through you into your personal relationships as He bears fruit through you.

8. If members did not participate in *MasterLife 1: The Disciple's Cross* or *MasterLife 2: The Disciple's Personality*, explain the purpose of the

Prayer-Covenant List. Direct them to a copy of the Prayer-Covenant List on page 143 of the member book. Tell them that they have permission to make additional copies of the list. Explain that members will record on their lists names, dates, and answers to prayers. Ask them to begin doing this now as they think of family members who need to know Christ.

Closure (5 minutes)

9. Announce the time and place for Group Session 1.

10. Stand and join hands in a prayer of dismissal. Pray on behalf of group members, especially as each person begins to think about family members who do not know Christ.

11. Express gratitude for each member, and ask them to pray for you as you seek to lead them in the days ahead.

AFTER THE SESSION

❑ Before the next group session pray specifically for each member.

❑ Call all members and encourage them in the study of the first week's material. Answer questions they may have, and encourage any who seem to need it. Thank each member for his or her commitment to the group.

❑ If anyone expresses doubt about joining the *MasterLife* group permanently, consider others to take their place. Ask all new members to complete "Overcoming the Enemy" before the next session. They will easily be able to start week 1. New members should not join the group after Group Session 1.

❑ Use the following questions to evaluate your leadership.

- Was I thoroughly prepared?
- Was my presentation clear?
- Did I follow the leader guide?
- Did I provide positive leadership?
- Was I a servant leader?
- Did I create a group environment?
- Did I help members communicate with each other?
- Do members understand the purpose of the study?
- Was I enthusiastic about how God will use *MasterLife* in members' lives and our church?

❑ Read "Before the Session" for the first group session to evaluate the amount of preparation you will need. At the top of the first page of Group Session 1 material, record when you will prepare.

❑ Carefully study week 2 and do all the exercises in the member book. You will preview week 2 for members during session 1.

One-to-One Study Plan

PART 1

1. Follow directions for the Standard Plan during the introductory time. Use this opportunity to discover needs and to help meet them. Allow the person to interact and ask questions as you talk together rather than your monopolizing the conversation. Be a friend.

2. Follow the Standard Plan for giving an overview of the material in *MasterLife 3: The Disciple's Victory.*

3. Follow the Standard Plan for referencing the Disciple's Cross and the Disciple's Personality. Share with the member how you have used the Disciple's Cross and the Disciple's Personality in your own life. You may have time to ask the member to give his or her presentations if he or she studied *MasterLife 1: The Disciple's Cross* or *MasterLife 2: The Disciple's Personality,* or you as leader may give them. A third option is to watch the video together while you point out significant actions during the presentation.

PART 2

Present the material related to the Spiritual Armor. Explain that he or she will learn the presentation by adding new material each week. The member will be expected to present the Spiritual Armor in his or her own words at the end of the study. Share with the member how you have used the Spiritual Armor to benefit your life. Follow the Standard Plan for explaining week 1 assignments.

GROUP SESSION 1

Overcoming the Enemy

Session Goals

By the end of this session, members will be able to demonstrate their commitment to *MasterLife* by …

- stating their goals for their study of *MasterLife 3: The Disciple's Victory;*
- explaining the Helmet of Salvation part of the Spiritual Armor;
- praying for family and friends that other group members mentioned as being in their circles of influence;
- saying from memory 1 John 4:4;
- describing the three types of strongholds that form the battleground for spiritual warfare;
- explaining the steps in how to demolish strongholds;
- completing the assignments for week 1.

Standard Plan

BEFORE THE SESSION

- ❏ Review the introduction and complete the learning activities for week 1 of *MasterLife 3: The Disciple's Victory* in order to conduct this week's group activities.
- ❏ To stay ahead of the group, carefully study week 2 and do all the learning activities in the member book. You will preview week 2 for the members at the end of this session.
- ❏ Find a quiet place and time to pray for group members by name. Ask the Lord to give you wisdom to prepare for and lead the session.
- ❏ Read "During the Session."
- ❏ List several immediate family members or relatives on your Relational-Witnessing Chart (p. 143 in the member book) so you are prepared to discuss this with group members.
- ❏ Arrange for refreshments to be served at the beginning of the session or at the break.
- ❏ Arrange chairs in a circle for everyone in the group.
- ❏ Have pens or pencils and extra blank paper on hand for the session.
- ❏ Plan to stay within the times given for each activity. The maximum time suggested is 45 or 60 minutes for each part. You may want to print an agenda with the subjects and times listed. This will guide the group and allow members to help the group stay on a schedule.
- ❏ Have name tags ready for members to learn each other's names.

❑ Group Session 2 requires that each member receive a witnessing booklet such as *How to Have a Full and Meaningful Life*. Determine the booklet you will provide and secure it in time for session 2.

Remember that allowing members to share freely is far more important than sticking legalistically to a plan you develop for the group session. Group members sometimes arrive at a session eager to tell about something that happened in their lives during the week related to that week's content. Be sensitive to this need, and be flexible. Allow God to work in your group. Provide opportunities for everyone to respond during the session.

DURING THE SESSION

PART 1 (45/60 minutes)

Introduction (10/15 minutes)
1. Welcome each person and point members to the refreshments. Tell them how glad you are they are participating in *MasterLife*. Let everyone visit informally until time to begin.

2. Begin promptly. Remind the group that you will begin and end each session on time. If group members want to fellowship or have additional discussions after the sessions, they may do so, but they can count on you to be prompt.

3. If your group members were together for *MasterLife 2: The Disciple's Personality* and therefore did not participate in the Introductory Session, give a brief overview of the material and course goals for *MasterLife 3: The Disciple's Victory*. If they participated in the Introductory Session, skip the overview.

4. Introduce any new members of the group. Ask them to give one fact that will help others remember their names. Ask group members to sign the covenant for *MasterLife 3: The Disciple's Victory*. If members for some reason did not participate in the *MasterLife 2: The Disciple's Personality* and are starting with book 3, they may not know the purpose and importance of the covenant. Explain it at this time.

5. Ask each member to give a brief statement of his or her goals for this study. Call the group to prayer. Invite volunteers to say sentence prayers asking God to help group members achieve their goals.

Prayer Time (10/15 minutes)
6. Tell your experience of how you used the Spiritual Armor in prayer during the past week. Then ask volunteers to share their experiences.

7. Review "Principles of Conversational Prayer" on page 41 of book 2. Remind members that they first learned to pray conversationally if they studied *MasterLife 2: The Disciple's Personality*. Show them how prayer partners can pray conversationally. Say, Many married couples have discovered that their prayer life together is more meaningful if they take turns leading in conversational prayer. One night the husband leads in the subjects prayed for, and the wife follows by praying for each of the same subjects. The next night the wife leads, mentioning the subjects in prayer, and the husband follows by praying for each subject. This practice allows each partner the same opportunity to pray. It also improves communication between husband and wife. Try this during the coming week. If you are not married, this same approach can be helpful for close friends who regularly pray together. Let's pray conversationally in groups of four.

"Overcoming the Enemy" (25/30 minutes)
Choose from the following list appropriate questions and activities for your group. Watch your time and reserve an adequate amount to make next week's assignments.

8. Discuss the question, Why do Christians need to be prepared for spiritual warfare? Ask a volunteer to describe a time when he or she experienced spiritual warfare. Ask another volunteer to describe a time when he or she experienced a victory in Christ after a battle with Satan.

9. Ask a volunteer to define *stronghold*. (*A stronghold is an idea, a thought process, a habit, or an addiction through which Satan has the advantage in a person's life.*) Ask a volunteer to share about a personal stronghold in which he or she struggles with Satan.

10. Ask members to respond to the statement, You are behind enemy lines—vulnerable to attack at any time. Ask volunteers to describe a recent local, national, or world event or occurrence in which they believe Satan has been active.

11. Ask a member to define *ideological stronghold*. Ask a volunteer to share about an ideological stronghold in which he or she is aware of Satan's influence.

12. Ask a member to define *cosmic stronghold*. Ask a volunteer to share about a cosmic stronghold in which he or she is aware of Satan's influence.

13. Ask a volunteer to share about a time in which he or she has tried to use the world's weapons in the attack against Satan. Ask another member to share about a time when he or she has used one of the spiritual weapons God gives us to fight Satan.

14. Ask members which role or scheme Satan uses most often to tempt or try them. (See the verses and exercise on p. 11 in day 1.)

15. Ask a member to read Matthew 4:1-11 and summarize how Jesus defeated Satan in the temptations in the wilderness.

16. Lead members to discuss "How to Demolish a Stronghold" on pages 24-25. Ask volunteers to explain each of the five points.

Take a stand-up break. Invite participants to help themselves to refreshments.

PART 2 (45/60 minutes)

Demolishing Personal Spiritual Strongholds (5/10 minutes)
1. Pair members with persons other than their spouses. Ask members to share in pairs about a personal stronghold they identified as needing to be demolished and how they are working to demolish that stronghold. Ask each person to pray that God will help the other person use the spiritual weapons Christ provides to demolish personal spiritual strongholds. Encourage members to check each other's assignments during this time period.

Guide to Thanksgiving (15 minutes)
2. Briefly summarize your experiences this week in using "Guide to Thanksgiving" in your prayer time. Invite members to share their experiences in giving thanks to God.

3. Highlight the difference between "Guide to Thanksgiving," which members studied this week, and "Guide to Praise," in next week's work. Say, "Guide to Praise" focuses more on who God is than on the things God does for us, which is the essence of "Guide to Thanksgiving." Let's pause and pray prayers of thanksgiving.

The Spiritual Armor (15/20 minutes)
4. Remind group members that through the Spiritual Armor they are expanding prayer and the Word of God, or the vertical bar of the Disciple's Cross. Tell them they are building on the inner victory they learned to have in *MasterLife 2: The Disciple's Personality* with the outer victory they can have when they use the spiritual weapons Christ has given them. Give a brief overview of the Spiritual Armor.

5. Instruct each person to present to another member in his or her own words the Helmet of Salvation part of the Spiritual Armor. If they give most of the ideas correctly, the partners should fill in the horizontal line on the diamond beside "Minister to Others" in "My Walk with the

Master This Week." Members are not expected to have learned the rest of the presentation. The Spiritual Armor is to be mastered a section at a time over the course of the study. Encourage members to use any extra time to check other assignments. If some members did not give most of the ideas correctly in this presentation, show the video presentation of the Spiritual Armor or loan it to them to refresh their memories.

6. Preview the Breastplate of Righteousness part of the Spiritual Armor presentation. Show how it fits the overall context of the Spiritual Armor. Say, You are not expected to know the entire presentation yet; you will continue to add elements in succeeding weeks. This is not the order of the pieces of armor in the presentation because we are learning them in the week the material relates to that piece of the armor.

Next Week's Assignments (5/10 minutes)
7. Ask members to look at "My Walk with the Master This Week" for week 2 on page 27 in *MasterLife 3: The Disciple's Victory*. Review the specific assignments. Remind them again that as they complete an assignment, they are to draw a vertical line through the diamond. A fellow member verifying their work during Group Session 2 will draw a horizontal line through the diamond to form a cross.

8. Preview the content of week 2 briefly. Ask members to complete the activities in the daily study "Truth and Faith" before the next session.

9. Call attention to the assignment in which members are asked to write prayer promises that apply to the requests on their Prayer-Covenant Lists. Urge them to be alert to promises from God's Word as they read from it during their daily quiet time.

10. Point out that members are also asked to write on their Prayer-Covenant List the names of people they know who are not saved. Encourage them to pray without ceasing for unsaved persons and to continually look for opportunities to relate to them. Remind members that they are to continue to reach out to non-Christians.

11. Explain the need to have a prayer partner. Members may continue praying with the same person they have if they have been involved in *MasterLife*, or they may enlist another prayer partner. Encourage them to pray in person or on the telephone with the partner each week.

12. Point out "Guide to Praise," which group members will use during the coming week. Urge them to use it during their prayer time.

Closure (5 minutes)
13. Stand and join hands for a prayer of dismissal. Ask volunteers to voice one-sentence prayers. Ask each person praying to pray especially for members as they relate to non-Christians during the next week.

14. Suggest that group members encourage each other between weekly sessions. Express gratitude that you are part of the group, and request members' prayers for you as you undertake to serve them during the weeks that follow.

AFTER THE SESSION
❑ Before the next group session pray for each member specifically.
❑ Call all group members and encourage them in their study. Answer any questions they may have. Thank each member for his or her commitment to the group.
❑ Use the following questions to evaluate your leadership.
  • Was I thoroughly prepared?
  • Was my presentation clear?
  • Did I follow the leader guide?
  • Did I provide positive leadership?
  • Was I a servant leader?
  • Did I create a group environment?
  • Did I help members communicate with each other?
  • Do members understand the purpose of the study?
  • Was I enthusiastic about how God will use *MasterLife* in members' lives and our church?
❑ Read "Before the Session" for Group Session 2 to evaluate the amount of preparation you will need. At the top of the first page of Group Session 2 material, record when you will prepare.
❑ Carefully study week 3 and do all the exercises in the member book. You will preview week 3 for members during session 3.

Split-Session Plan

1. The Split-Session Plan begins with Group Session 2. Session 1 should be conducted as a single session.

2. Preview next week's assignment. Assign days 1–3 of the study "Truth and Faith" for the first week of session 2 and days 4–5 for the second week of session 2.

One-to-One Study Plan

PART 1
1. Follow directions for the Standard Plan during the introductory time. Use this opportunity to learn more about the person you are working with and how you can best help him or her. Avoid lecturing to the person; allow him or her to discover answers as you work together.

2. Ask the person to quote 1 John 4:4, the verse he or she memorized during week 1. Check other assignments completed.

3. Explore the person's understanding of spiritual warfare, and share your insights. Share with the person about times when you tried to fight spiritual battles on your own, and ask him or her to share experiences of trying to fight Satan without relying on God. Each of you share about a victory you have experienced in relying on God in a spiritual battle.

4. Explore the person's understanding of the three types of strong-holds—personal, ideological, and cosmic. Discuss your responses to each type of stronghold. Share about a time when you believe that Satan has been active in recent national or international events.

5. Discuss ways you feel you can keep the concept of strategic spiritual warfare in its proper perspective.

6. Share ways you have used the Bible to help you fight a spiritual battle. Ask the person to share his or her experiences.

7. Because you are working one-to-one, you can spend more time helping the person understand the principles of overcoming the strongholds that Satan establishes in your life. Tell your own experiences in using the spiritual weapons or character traits God has given you to demolish these strongholds.

PART 2

1. Ask the person to present the Helmet of Salvation part of the Spiritual Armor.

2. Follow the Standard Plan for explaining week 2 assignments.

GROUP SESSION 2

Truth and Faith

> **Session Goals**
>
> By the end of this session, members will be able to demonstrate their progress toward *MasterLife* goals by …
> - sharing prayer promises God has given them that apply to items on their Prayer-Covenant Lists;
> - completing assignments for week 2;
> - explaining the Breastplate of Righteousness part of the Spiritual Armor;
> - defining *truth* and *faith* and their relationship to each other;
> - praying, using principles of conversational prayer;
> - praying for people group members know who are not saved.

Standard Plan

BEFORE THE SESSION

❑ Review week 2 and read and complete the learning activities for week 3 of *MasterLife 3: The Disciple's Victory*.

❑ Pray daily for each member of the group. Ask the Lord to give you wisdom to prepare for and lead the group session.

❑ Master this week's material in the leader guide.

❑ Review the goals for this session.

❑ Check with the host or hostess to be sure he or she is ready for the group this week.

❑ Arrange the meeting place so that members can sit in a circle.

❑ Have pens or pencils and extra blank paper on hand for the session.

❑ Be prepared to share about your experiences in recording prayer promises that apply to your requests on your Prayer-Covenant List.

❑ Review "How to Listen to God's Word" on page 33 in the member book so you can share highlights of it with the group.

❑ Begin making plans for the Prayer Workshop that follows the study of *MasterLife 3: The Disciple's Victory*. Be prepared to give suggestions about the time and place, or during this session announce to members these details if they have already been determined. A retreat setting is ideal, but meeting at church may be best for the group in terms of convenience and expense. Most churches have enough space for each person to be alone in a room. Most houses are not large enough for a *MasterLife* group and have too many distractions on a Saturday or a Sunday when the half day of prayer is planned. A Saturday from 8:00 a.m. to noon is preferable. In addition, if group members agree, they could have lunch together, followed by a time of group prayer, sharing, and fun in the afternoon. They need a minimum of three hours of prayer time in a place where they can be alone. The total group session requires a minimum of four hours.

❑ Provide one witnessing booklet for each member for use during the session.

DURING THE SESSION

PART 1 (45/60 minutes)

Introduction (25/30 minutes)
1. Greet members as they arrive. Begin on time. Be alert to any signs of progress or any problems members may be facing. Ask for special prayer requests. Open the session with prayer.

2. Ask members to pair with someone other than their spouses to check each other's work on "My Walk with the Master This Week." Instruct them to ask the other person if he or she did the assignment. The persons verifying may ask to see the work done. Tell them to make certain members quote memory verses correctly before this activity is marked.

3. Ask each pair to share with each other the promises God has given them that apply to requests on their Prayer-Covenant Lists.

4. Join together as a total group to pray, using "Guide to Praise." Invite members to share names of lost persons for whom they are praying. Spend time in prayer for these individuals. Talk about how being part of the body of Christ helps us in times of spiritual warfare.

"Truth and Faith" (20/30 minutes)
5. Remind members to complete all the learning activities and learn the material before they attend the group session. The purpose of discussing the material in the group session is to reflect on it, explore the subject further, and apply it.

6. Ask members to define *truth,* based on the material "Truth and Faith." Make sure the definition includes God's revelation of Himself through Jesus and the written Word.

7. Ask, Why can Christians know the truth? (*They are born of the Spirit and have been given the Word.*)

8. Say, In the Disciple's Personality you learned that the soul processes information through the mind, will, and emotions (point them out on the poster you prepared in the Introductory Session). The soul receives information through three sources, each beginning with *S*. What are

they? (*Senses, which come through the body; Satan, who comes through flesh; and Spirit, who comes through our human spirit.*) The soul (self) can work only with the information it receives. If all sources are accepted as equally valid, the soul (self) becomes confused and is susceptible to error. Would someone be willing to rank these three sources—the senses, Satan, the Spirit—in order of validity and tell why you ranked them that way? (*The Holy Spirit reveals pure truth. The senses reveal physical information, but it can be true or false. Satan is the father of lies and distorts the truth.*)

9. Say, Faith should be based on truth.
   - Ask, What happens if faith is based on data from the senses? (*It can be wrong because the senses can be deceived. Examples are magicians' tricks, mirages, and psychosomatic illnesses. If faith is based on pure data, it is no longer faith but knowledge.*)
   - Ask, Why is it wrong to base faith on interpretations whose sole basis is the mind, the will, and the emotions? (*The mind, the will, and the emotions are subject to great error.*)
   - Ask, Why are the mind, the will, and the emotions inadequate to interpret data? (*The mind has only partial data. It is influenced greatly by the will and the emotions. The will can believe what it wishes whether it is true or not. Emotions are likely to believe what will please them.*)
   - Ask, What happens if faith is based on the written truth revealed by the Holy Spirit? (*It is valid and comes to pass. Of course, it may be misinterpreted if the mind, will, and emotions work in conflict with the truth rather than in harmony with the truth.*)
   - Ask, Why is it important to be filled with the Spirit when you interpret the Word? (*So you will rightly divide the Word of truth [see 2 Tim. 2:15] and not twist it [see 2 Cor. 4:2]*).

10. Read 2 Timothy 3:16-17. Ask, Who inspired the Word? (*Holy Spirit*) Through what means do you think the Holy Spirit wants to communicate the truth to you today? (*God's Word*)

11. Ask, How do you define *faith*? (*Faith is not hoping but trusting in God's revealed Word.*) Where does faith come from? (*Romans 10:17 says from hearing the Word of God.*) How does faith manifest itself? (*By acting on the basis of the Word.*)

12. Use the following story to illustrate faith. A college student from a warm southern state is attending his first semester of school in Alaska. Early in the year the hard, cold winter sets in. His parents, in a rush of concern, buy him an extra heavy coat and send it by mail. They call him to let him know a package is on the way. His father says, "We have sent you a coat. Pick it up at the post office addressed to you, general delivery." The student says, "Thanks." "Thanks for what?" "The coat, of

course." He leaves the dorm without a coat and someone says to him, "Man, you need a coat." He replies, "No, I don't. I have one." Ask, How can the student say that? (*He believes his father.*) He has not seen or felt the coat. But he has the assurance that it is real even though he can't see or touch it. That assurance has come to him by the word of his father.[1] Emphasize the assurance we can feel when we ask for something that the Heavenly Father has revealed He wants to do for us or in us.

13. Say, The Old Testament word for *faith* was *faithfulness*. Ask, How did the heroes in Hebrews 11 demonstrate their faith? (*By acting on the basis of what God told them, without having proof.*)

14. Give a personal illustration of your believing a Spirit-illuminated Scripture and of God's honoring your faith. It may have been your believing John 3:16 for salvation.

15. Close part 1 with prayer, asking God to help everyone in the group learn how to pray in faith based on the God's Word.

Take a stand-up break. Invite participants to help themselves to refreshments.

PART 2 (45/60 minutes)

Working in Pairs (20/25 minutes)
1. Ask group members to share with a partner about personal strongholds they identified this week as needing to be demolished. Invite each person to tell how he or she is working to demolish that stronghold. Ask members to pray that God will help the other person use the spiritual weapons Christ has given them to demolish personal spiritual strongholds.

2. Instruct each person to present to the other in his or her own words the Breastplate of Righteousness part of the Spiritual Armor. They do not need to memorize the Scriptures that accompany the presentation, but ideally, they need to know how to find the verses or use them as references. If they give most of the ideas correctly, their partner should fill in the horizontal line on the diamond beside "Minister to Others" in "My Walk with the Master This Week." Members are not expected to have learned the rest of the presentation. Remind them that the Spiritual Armor is to be mastered a section at a time over a six-week period. Encourage members to use any extra time to check on other assignments. If several members did not give most of the ideas correctly in this presentation, show the video presentation of the Spiritual Armor or loan it to them to refresh their memories.

3. Distribute a witnessing booklet to each member. Explain to members that they will use this booklet with someone when they want to go beyond the content of their personal Christian testimony. Tell them that beginning in week 3 and for the two weeks thereafter, they will study suggestions of how to introduce the booklet when they witness to someone. You may want to review some of these suggestions in weeks 3–5 and use them as you train group members.

The Spiritual Armor (10/20 minutes)
4. Preview for members the Sword of the Spirit part of the Spiritual Armor. Explain to members that as they learn the Sword of the Spirit part of the Spiritual Armor, they will also learn an additional presentation that teaches how to get a grasp on God's Word. This is known as God's Word in Your Heart and Hand (pp. 132-4).

5. Practice giving the level 1 demonstration in God's Word in Your Heart and Hand. Encourage members to remember in the most simple terms what the various fingers mean as well as be able to explain the other parts of the illustration in their own words. They will have an opportunity to explain the illustration to each other in next week's group session. Suggest that they may want to view the videotape.

Next Week's Assignments and Closure (5 minutes)
6. Ask members to look at the assignments in "My Walk with the Master This Week" for week 3 on page 43 in the member book.

7. Call attention to "Guide to Confession and Forgiveness" (pp. 54-55) and encourage members to use it in their prayer time during the week ahead.

8. Brief group members on plans being developed for the upcoming Prayer Workshop.

9. Deal with any problems or questions members may have. Praise them for their progress and encourage them to keep up the good work.

10. Announce the meeting place for next week. Close with prayer. Ask God to help each member in the spiritual warfare that confronts them in the week ahead.

AFTER THE SESSION
❏ Evaluate the session by listing what you believe was effective. Consider ways to improve future sessions.
❏ Evaluate the response of individual members to the teaching on truth and faith. Talk with any members who you think need personal help at this time.

❏ Look for opportunities to praise members sincerely, particularly any who may be experiencing problems. Offer your help as needed.

❏ Take one or more members witnessing. Don't ask them to do anything they are not experienced in doing. The purpose is for them to observe. Before each visit, tell them what you expect to find and do. After the visit, talk about what you did and did not do and why you conducted the visit as you did. Use the Gospel in Hand presentation (member book 4, p. 128) when you witness each week so members can be familiar with it before they are asked to learn it. By the end of the study you should have taken everyone in the group with you at least once.

❏ Read "Before the Session" for Group Session 3. Evaluate the amount of preparation you will need for the session. At the top of the first page of Group Session 3, record when you will prepare.

❏ Carefully study week 4 and do all the exercises in the member book. You will preview week 4 for members during session 3.

❏ Follow up on arrangements for the Prayer Workshop. Enlist others to help you as necessary.

Split-Session Plan

FIRST WEEK

1. Use activity 1 in part 2 of the Standard Plan as your first activity. Talk about demolishing personal spiritual strongholds. Save the parts about prayer promises and praying for unsaved persons until the second week of the split session. Members learn about these during the second week.

2. Lead the content review of "Truth and Faith." Review items 5–11 only. Items 12–15 pertain to material members will study next week. You will need to adjust the times each week to keep them within the 45/60 minute framework.

3. Preview next week's assignments. Call attention to the fact that your group is using the Split-Session Plan. This means that members will check off only those assignments that pertain to the material they have studied that week. For example, members were assigned only days 1–3 for the first week of this session. Therefore, they would not be able to check off the assignment about prayer promises because that assignment does not appear until day 4. The other assignments will be done the following week. During this preview time, review only the assignments they will be responsible for next week.

SECOND WEEK

1. Arrive early. Begin the session on time. Use shorter times for each activity as necessary.

2. Ask members to share briefly about the assignment to write on their Prayer-Covenant Lists prayer promises that apply to requests. Then ask volunteers to share the names of people they know who are not saved. Invite members to pray short prayers for these people. Tell them that you will pray last. Lead in prayer when time has expired. This period should not be a full-length prayer meeting.

3. Pair members with persons other than their spouses. Each member of the pair should check the other person's "My Walk with the Master This Week." The boxes with the vertical marks should be verified and crossed off. Invite each person in the pair to quote 2 Timothy 3:16-17. These verses should be quoted accurately by each member before the assignment is marked off.

4. Lead the content review of "Truth and Faith." Spend a brief amount of time reviewing what members have already learned during the first week. Ask volunteers to summarize important points from last week's study. Then move to items 12–15.

5. Practice presenting the Breastplate of Righteousness part of the Spiritual Armor. Follow instructions in the Standard Plan for making the presentation.

6. Preview next week's assignments. This will not take as much time to explain because of the members' experience the previous week. Assign members days 1-3 in the material "Rely on God's Word." Members are to complete only assignments that pertain to the material for this week. Close in prayer, praying that each member will have victory in spiritual warfare in his or her life during the week ahead.

One-to-One Study Plan

Follow instructions in the Standard Plan. Make the following adjustments for the one-to-one relationship.

PART 1
1. Review the content in "Truth and Faith." Be frank about the battle you have in being confronted with Satan's lies as opposed to following God's truths. Ask the person in what area he or she has problems.

2. Share experiences you have had in finding prayer promises that apply to the requests on your Prayer-Covenant List. Ask the person to share experiences he or she has had in this area. Pray conversationally with the person you are discipling.

PART 2
1. Introduce the Sword of the Spirit part of the Spiritual Armor and God's Word in Your Heart and Hand. Do this by presenting each. Ask the person to note anything that is different from your presentation and the one in the member book.

2. Preview next week's assignments. Explain how to use the witnessing booklet. Describe experiences you have had using this booklet or another gospel presentation with an unsaved person.

———
[1]Thomas D. Elliff, *Praying for Others* (Nashville: Broadman Press, 1979), 23-24.

GROUP SESSION 3
Rely on God's Word

Session Goals
By the end of this session, members will be able to demonstrate their progress toward *MasterLife* goals by ...
- completing assignments for week 3;
- explaining the Sword of the Spirit part of the Spiritual Armor;
- praying for group members' requests about lost persons listed on their Relational-Witnessing Charts;
- sharing their experiences using the witnessing booklet;
- describing the four areas for which Scripture is useful;
- identifying how Scripture has been useful in their lives in those four areas.

Standard Plan

BEFORE THE SESSION
- ❏ Review week 3 and read and complete the learning activities for week 4 of *MasterLife 3: The Disciple's Victory*.
- ❏ Call members who are having problems completing assignments to ask them how they are doing this week and to encourage them.
- ❏ Master this week's material in the leader guide.
- ❏ Review the goals for this session.
- ❏ Check with the host or hostess to be sure he or she is ready for the group this week.
- ❏ Arrange the meeting place so that members can sit in a circle.
- ❏ Have pens or pencils and extra blank paper on hand for the session.

❑ Continue to make plans for the Prayer Workshop that follows Group Session 6.

❑ Use "Guide to Confession and Forgiveness" during your personal prayer time before you use it with the group.

❑ Look for opportunities for sharing the witnessing booklet or another gospel booklet with an unsaved person. Be prepared to share your experience with group members. Invite one or two members to go with you to witness to lost persons.

❑ If members do not appear to be keeping up with their assignments using the Standard Plan or will not be able to give the Spiritual Armor successfully by Group Session 6, extend week 4 assignments over the next two weeks. To do this, use the Split-Session Plan for session 4. Decide now so you can give the proper instructions for the plan you will use this week.

DURING THE SESSION

PART 1 (45/60 minutes)

Introduction (25/30 minutes)

1. Begin the session on time even if all members are not present. During this time ask members to share progress on overcoming any problems they have experienced in their work.

2. Ask members for reports on their experiences in sharing the witnessing booklet with an unsaved person. Tell your experience first; then invite others to share. Ask members to mention names they are praying for in their circles of influence. Ask each member to pray a sentence prayer for the person on his or her right pertaining to request the person mentioned during this sharing time.

3. Invite volunteers to share experiences in using "Guide to Confession and Forgiveness" during their prayer times this week.

4. Ask group members to pair up and quote Psalm 1:2-3 to each other. Encourage husbands and wives not to pair up. As members work in pairs, instruct them to verify each other's "My Walk with the Master This Week." Remind them to mark the horizontal line in the members' diamond boxes after verifying completed work. Encourage the pairs to share their strong and weak points in completing the assignments.

"Rely on God's Word" (25/30 minutes)
Choose from the following list appropriate questions and activities for your group's study. Do not exceed the time allowance.

5. Ask a member to read or quote 2 Timothy 3:16-17. Ask, What does "All Scripture is God-breathed" mean?

6. Invite a volunteer to share about a time when he or she tried to rely on sources other than God's Word to provide guidance.

7. Ask, With which of the four ways that Scripture equips you—teaching, rebuking, correcting, and training in righteousness—have you had the most experience? Or, ask members to tell about their most recent experience with one of these four ways. Ask volunteers to share their answers.

8. Invite a volunteer to share a time when he or she has truly delighted in God's Word—had an actual hunger and thirst for the Scriptures and reacted exuberantly to them. Quote Psalm 1:2-3 together.

9. Ask members to recall times when proper teaching in God's Word prevented them from making harmful decisions.

10. Ask members to share about times when a verse of Scripture convicted them that they were headed in the wrong direction.

11. Ask members to describe the difference between the Scripture's roles in rebuking and correcting. (*Rebuking involves making you aware that you are traveling the opposite direction than you should be going. Correcting involves a slight change of direction to get back on course before rebuke is necessary.*)

12. Ask, How is the instruction in the Bible more than just a set of how-to rules? (*The Bible teaches how to live life. It is involved in teaching moral character—of training in Christlikeness. It is not merely a set of do's and don'ts.*) Discuss the situations on page 51 when rebuke is commended.

13. Ask members to share about times when they have found the Bible useful in instructing how to act in a specific situation. Discuss the three instances of correction on page 53, day 4.

14. Ask members to respond to the following statement: Being well-grounded in the Word of God guarantees that I will never have problems and that I will not sin. (*Possible response: Being equipped with Scripture is no guarantee against problems, but it does mean you will be able to rely on God's guidance in troubled times.*)

15. Read this statement from day 5: "As a Christian you are not left to guess which way is right. Again and again the Bible instructs you in the practical, day-to-day ways to live." Invite a volunteer to share a time when he or she found this to be true.

16. Ask whether anyone did a study on a Bible character (see "How to Study God's Word," p. 46). If so, ask that person to tell what he or she

learned and the value of this type of study. If no one did this, share the one you studied.

17. Ask members to pray. Lead the group in a prayer asking God to help members rely on God's Word in all times and in all situations.

Take a stand-up break. Invite participants to help themselves to refreshments.

PART 2 (45/60 minutes)

The Spiritual Armor (10/15 minutes)
1. Ask each member to pair with a person he or she has not yet worked with. Instruct members to present the Sword of the Spirit part of the Spiritual Armor to their partners. Remind them that the Spiritual Armor is to be mastered a section at a time over a six-week period. If anyone did not give most of the ideas correctly in this presentation, loan him or her the video presentation of the Spiritual Armor to review.

Demolishing Spiritual Strongholds (5 minutes)
2. Ask a volunteer to share what personal spiritual strongholds are being demolished in his or her life and what spiritual weapons he or she is using in the process. Pray a prayer of thanksgiving for what this person has shared and for the growth others have experienced.

God's Word in Your Heart and Hand (15/20 minutes)
3. With members in pairs, instruct them to practice giving to each other the demonstration (level 1) of God's Word in Your Heart and Hand. If they give most of the ideas correctly, the partners make a horizontal mark in the diamond box in "My Walk with the Master This Week."

4. Demonstrate level 2 of God's Word in Your Heart and Hand (see pp. 133-4). On the chalkboard or poster paper draw the hand with the Scriptures on it. Remind members that they will be able to give the presentation by the end of week 6. You may quote or assign the verses to read. You may also choose to use the videotape in this demonstration.

Next Week's Assignments and Closure (10/15 minutes)
5. Call attention to the Praying in Faith form on page 139. Tell members they will find elements of this form interspersed throughout week 4 to make it easier to study and answer as they read. Explain that in day 2 they will describe a problem they are facing and will then use various elements of the Praying in Faith form to work through that problem throughout the week. Explain to members that they will use the Praying in Faith form as it appears in its entirety with later problems they face. Assure members that as they use this method consistently,

they will experience God communicating truth to them and the blessing of praying in faith.

6. Ask members to look at "My Walk with the Master This Week" for week 4 on page 60 and review the specific assignments. Make sure they understand how to complete each assignment.

7. Briefly preview the content of week 4. Ask members to complete the material "Pray in Faith" before session 4.

8. Review with members the Shield of Faith part of the Spiritual Armor. By the end of the study they will be able to explain all of the Spiritual Armor in their own words.

9. Call attention to the assignment about continuing to write on your Relational-Witnessing Chart the names of non-Christians. Urge members to be on the lookout for opportunities to share their faith.

10. Ask whether members have any questions about the upcoming Prayer Workshop. Share any additional details you may have confirmed during the week.

11. Announce the time and place for the next session. Stand and join hands in a prayer of dismissal. Ask each member to voice a one-sentence prayer for the person on his or her right. Say, Ask God to help this member grow in his or her relationship with God.

AFTER THE SESSION

❑ Meet individually or in small groups with members who seem to be having special problems with demolishing personal spiritual strongholds in their lives. Pray with them about their problems.

❑ Encourage any members who may be lagging behind in their assignments. Help them with any problems. If necessary, enlist another member to help them.

❑ Take one or more members witnessing. You may want to visit some of the non-Christians they listed on their Relational-Witnessing Charts. Model by using your personal testimony.

❑ Pray for each member, using specific verses as the basis of your prayers. You may want to share with each person the verse you claimed for him or her. This could be done by card, telephone, or personal contact. Members will be motivated and helped by your visualization of expectations as stated in the verse.

❑ Read "Before the Session" for Group Session 4 to evaluate the amount of time you will need to prepare for the next group session. Record at the top of the first page of the Group Session 4 material when you will prepare.

❑ Carefully study week 5 and do all the exercises in the member book. You will preview week 5 for members during session 4.

Split-Session Plan

FIRST WEEK

1. Ask members to discuss ways they are demolishing the personal spiritual strongholds they identified. Invite volunteers to pray short prayers of thanksgiving for the victories the members cited. Pray a brief prayer and invite others to pray also.

2. Ask members to work in pairs to check each other's assignments in "My Walk with the Master This Week."

3. Lead the content review of "Rely on God's Word." Review items 5-10 in the Standard Plan. Items 11-17 pertain to materials members will study next week.

4. Preview next week's assignments. Assign members days 4–5 in the material. During this preview time, review only the assignments that they will be responsible for next week.

SECOND WEEK

1. Ask members to share ways they have begun to use the witnessing booklet in dealing with unsaved persons. Share your experiences in using this booklet. Then ask members to share names of unsaved people that they wrote on their Relational-Witnessing Charts. Ask members to pray about items they shared.

2. Ask members to work in pairs to check off each other's "My Walk with the Master This Week" and mark the horizontal mark in the members' diamond boxes after verifying completed work.

3. Ask pairs to give to each other the Sword of the Spirit part of the Spiritual Armor and level 1 of God's Word in Your Heart and Hand.

4. Lead the study "Rely on God's Word." Spend about three minutes reviewing what members learned during the first week of this study. Ask volunteers to summarize important points from last week's study. Then move to items 11-17 in the Standard Plan.

5. Preview next week's assignments. Follow the instructions on the Standard Plan about previewing assignments. Assign members days 1–3 in the study "Pray in Faith." Members are to complete only assignments that pertain to the material they study this week.

6. Close in prayer, using "Guide to Confession and Forgiveness" during your prayer time.

One-to-One Plan

PART 1
Follow instructions for the Standard Plan. Since you are relating to only one person, you can give special help during this time. Help the person share personal spiritual strongholds he or she has difficulty demolishing so that you can help identify character traits or spiritual weapons to use in this warfare. Share solutions that have worked for you.

PART 2
Follow instructions for the Standard Plan. Help your partner learn the Spiritual Armor concepts so he or she can relate it in his or her own words. The goal is not to memorize a set of facts but to make this illustration real and personal so that the member can share from the heart how this armor is useful in spiritual warfare.

GROUP SESSION 4

Pray in Faith

Session Goals
By the end of this session, members will be able to demonstrate their progress toward *MasterLife* goals by ...
- stating how they are demolishing personal spiritual strongholds;
- completing assignments for week 4;
- presenting the Shield of Faith part of the Spiritual Armor;
- saying from memory 1 John 5:14-15;
- praying for unsaved close friends, neighbors, and coworkers of group members;
- stating the six steps for praying in faith;
- selecting a problem or need about which they want to pray;
- sharing times when they have linked prayer and God's Word.

Standard Plan

BEFORE THE SESSION
❑ Review week 4 and read and complete the learning activities for week 5 of *MasterLife 3: The Disciple's Victory.*

❑ Pray for each member of your group. Some may be discouraged as the amount of work to accomplish before a session increases. Ask God for guidance and encouragement in each member's life.

❑ Master this week's material in the leader guide.

❑ Review the goals for this session.

❑ Check with the host or hostess to be sure he or she is ready for the group this week.

❑ Arrange the meeting place so that members can sit in a circle.

❑ Have pens or pencils and extra blank paper on hand for the session.

❑ Review the memory verses to date to be sure that you know them.

❑ Use the Praying in Faith form in your own prayer time so you can report to members how you are working to solve a problem based on prayer and the Word.

❑ Make a poster or write on a chalkboard the following outline of the material on the Praying in Faith form.

GOD COMMUNICATES TRUTH TO ME

Abide in Christ

Abide in the Word

Allow the Holy Spirit to Lead You in Truth

I COMMUNICATE FAITH TO GOD

Ask According to God's Will

Accept God's Will in Faith

Act on the Basis of God's Word to You

❑ Survey the location selected for the Prayer Workshop. A room is needed for each participant. Be sure these are available and are heated or cooled. If you use an outdoor setting, be sure enough secluded sites are available for each person to have privacy. Identify the location of rest rooms so you can tell members.

❑ Organize your prayer journal as a model for members to see as you train them to prepare their prayer journals.

DURING THE SESSION

PART 1 (45/60 minutes)

Introduction (25/30 minutes)

1. Arrive early and greet members as they arrive. Be alert and available to discuss any questions they may have. Begin on time and with prayer.

2. Divide the group in half. Ask members to share in their groups reports on adding to their Relational-Witnessing Charts names of persons they know who are unsaved. Ask members to pray short prayers for the individuals that fellow group members have mentioned.

3. Pair members with persons other than their spouses. Ask members to check each other's "My Walk with the Master This Week." Encourage them to use any extra time to review memory verses.

4. Instruct everyone to come back together as one group. Share with the group your experiences of using the Praying in Faith form. Tell members about a problem you have to which you are applying the principles of prayer and the Word. Ask members to share their testimonies using your model as a guide.

"Pray in Faith" (20/30 minutes)
Choose from the following list appropriate questions and activities for your group's study. Do not feel that you have to use each question. Do not exceed the time allowance.

5. Ask members to explain the relationship of praying in faith to living in the Word.

6. Ask, Why is the prayer list titled Prayer-Covenant List? (*Because we are learning to ask on the basis of a promise or instruction from God and to make a covenant with Him.*)

7. Invite a member to explain what a covenant is. Discuss some of the covenants of the Bible. Ask, What are the stages of a covenant-making process? If we follow this process, what do we prevent? (*Our deciding what we want and trying to bargain with God to get it.*)

8. Ask, What are the three steps for God's communicating truth to you? Refer to the list that you have written on the poster or chalkboard.

9. Say, Purity of heart and obedience to God do not force God to give you anything you want. We can be sure we will get what we want only if God has revealed through His Word and Spirit that He wants to give us that thing. God answers when our wills coincide with His will. When our wills are different from God's will, He may do one of two things:
- God encourages us to ask for the right thing. Give this illustration. Say, Suppose you bought your 10-year-old child a bicycle for Christmas at a September sale. Several weeks before Christmas, your child begins to ask for a rifle. What do you do? Because you know what is best for him in this case, you subtly talk about all the benefits of a bicycle. You show him bicycles. You may even talk about or demonstrate to him the dangers of rifles. You continue to influence him and arrange circumstances until on his own he asks for a bicycle for Christmas. You are then free to give him the bicycle because he decided he wanted it and he asked you for it.

- God encourages us to do His will and trust Him for what is best for us. Give the illustration of how God dealt with Paul. Read 2 Corinthians 12:7-10 and ask the following questions.
  — Why was a messenger of Satan allowed to give Paul a thorn in the flesh? (*To keep him from being proud.*)
  — Did Paul ask for it to be taken away? (*Yes, three times.*)
  — Why did God not take it away? (*Because God wanted to teach Paul that through his weakness God could reveal His power.*)
  — Did Paul learn to pray the right prayer when God revealed His will? (Read v. 10.)

10. Invite members to comment on the following statement about Romans 8:28 from "Guide to Praying in Faith": "That does not mean that all things *are* good but that ultimately, God will work together all things to produce good."

11. Ask, What are the three steps for your communicating faith to God? Refer to the list you have written on the poster or the chalkboard.

12. Brainstorm reasons why God does not always answer the way we want Him to. (*Answers might include: It would not be best for us; it would require God to violate someone's will, or it would require Him to violate natural consequences brought about when the laws of nature are broken; we need to wait until later; it would not glorify God; God wants to develop a character trait in us.*) Ask, What would you do if a friend asked you to pray for something you felt would be wrong? When you pray for guidance, do you always do what you discern is God's will? Allow time for discussion.

13. Ask, Why do you think we do not have all God wills to give us? (*Because we often fail to ask for the things He wants us to have, or we ask with improper motives; read Jas. 4:2-3.*)

14. Invite a volunteer to share about a time when he or she acted after praying in faith even though the person couldn't see what the outcome would be.

15. Ask, Under what conditions should a person go through the six steps for finding God's will based on prayer and the Word? (*Use this exercise in the major problems and decisions you face. But if you get in the habit of daily living in the Word and praying in faith, this will help you make decisions with the direct leading of the Spirit.*)

16. Lead in prayer for guidance as members learn to pray in faith.

Take a stand-up break. Invite participants to help themselves to refreshments.

PART 2 (45/60 minutes)

Prayer Time (5 minutes)

1. Call the group together for prayer. Ask volunteers to share about opportunities they have had to use the witnessing booklet with someone who needs it. Ask if anyone has an update on any prayer requests that group members have mentioned so far during the study. Lead the group to pray short prayers related to the experiences or the prayer requests mentioned.

Demolishing Personal Spiritual Strongholds (5 minutes)

2. Share your experience of working on demolishing the personal spiritual stronghold of religious ritual. Ask group members to share their experiences in using a spiritual weapon to rid themselves of this stronghold. Pray a prayer of thanksgiving for what members have shared and for the growth that others have experienced.

Practice Presentations (10/15 minutes)

3. Ask members to work in pairs and present the Shield of Faith presentation to each other. Instruct each person to practice drawing the hand in God's Word in Your Heart and Hand (pp. 132-4) and writing the verses on it. Members are not expected to memorize the verses, but they should be able to find the verses and read them. If several members did not give most ideas correctly in this presentation, consider giving the entire presentation to the group again or showing the video presentation of the Spiritual Armor to refresh their memory.

Prayer Journal (15/25 minutes)

4. Call attention to "How to Develop Your Personal Prayer Journal" on page 87 in week 5. Explain the purpose of the personal prayer journal. After the explanation say, Several of you may be finding it difficult to be consistent in the weekly assignments without group monitoring and help. A prayer journal provides a framework for monitoring yourself. The journal also makes it possible to draw all the prayer resources in *MasterLife* together so they will be easier to use. Also, most of us need to clarify our life goals and manage our time and lives better. A personal prayer journal helps us do that. For those of you who studied *MasterLife 1: The Disciple's Cross*, let me remind you of "How to Use MasterTime" on page 88. You may want to include it in your personal prayer journal. We need to make prayer a ministry of the Lord for our church and for the world. One thing that will assist us in all of this will be the Prayer Workshop at the end of week 6.

5. Discuss the development of the personal prayer journal, using the explanation on pages 87–89 of the member book as a guide. Display your own personal prayer journal for members to see. Let them ask questions as needed. They will have two weeks to work on their journals before the Prayer Workshop.

Next Week's Assignments (15 minutes)

6. Present level 3 (p. 134) of God's Word in Your Heart and Hand. Refer to the videotape for an example of involving members in the illustrations. Tell members that they will be able to do the same thing by the end of next week's work. Preview the Gospel Shoes part of the Spiritual Armor that they will learn in week 5. Remind members that they will be able to give the entire Spiritual Armor presentation by the end of the last week.

7. Ask members to look at "My Walk with the Master This Week" on page 83 of week 5 and review the specific assignments. Make sure the members understand how to complete each assignment.

8. Briefly preview the content of week 5. Ask members to complete the daily material in "Look to Jesus" before Group Session 5.

9. Call attention to "Expanding Your Witness Circle" on page 105 of the member book. Note that the members will read this material and continue to add names to their Relational-Witnessing Charts. Explain that the witnessing booklet or another gospel booklet will give members a vehicle to use as they expand their witness circles.

10. Call attention to the fact that members will study life purpose and life goals in week 5. Explain the difference between the two. Say, A life purpose is an overarching objective for you to accomplish in your life. It provides direction for everyday activities and determines your priorities. A life goal is a specific objective for an important area of your life. Achieving your life goals should equal achieving your life purpose. Days 4 and 5 may take longer than usual. If you are rushed, you may want to complete your life goals during the Prayer Workshop.

11. Call attention to the assignment about using "Guide to Intercession" during members' prayer time the following week. Suggest that members intercede for the names they have written on their Relational-Witnessing Charts as they use the guide in their prayer time.

Closure (5 minutes)

12. Announce the meeting time and place for next week. Remind members about the Prayer Workshop and provide details.

13. Remind members of the importance of having each item checked off in "My Walk with the Master This Week" as soon as possible to keep these activities from accumulating at the end of the book. Offer individual help after the session if needed.

14. Divide into two groups for a closing conversational prayer.

AFTER THE SESSION

❑ Use the following questions to evaluate the group life.
  • Do members care for one another? Do they trust one another? Are they becoming more open with one another?
  • Are there blocks in communication?
  • Are spouses relating well as group members?
  • Are members responding well to my leadership?
  • Is the group becoming cliquish? Do I need to encourage members to keep reaching out?
  • Do some members show undesirable attitudes toward other members? Should I take them visiting and/or pair them up more often?
  • Are members helping disciple each other?
  • Do they see me as a growing disciple who is learning from them?

❑ Continue to invite members to go witnessing and ministering with you. Take them on church visitation or hospital calls.

❑ Call or see all members of the group this week to encourage, enable, or challenge them as needed. See if any need help completing assignments or working on their testimonies. Remember that you are their servant. Continue to look for opportunities to praise them.

❑ Pray for members. Remember their prayer requests.

❑ Read "Before the Session" for Group Session 5 to evaluate the amount of time you will need to prepare for the next group session. At the beginning of session 5 material, record when you will prepare.

❑ Carefully study week 6 and do all the exercises in the member book. You will preview week 6 for members during session 5.

Split-Session Plan

FIRST WEEK

1. Follow the Standard Plan for the small-group time of checking each other's work in "My Walk with the Master This Week" and of using the Praying in Faith form. Save the discussion of the Relational-Witnessing Chart until part 2 since members will study it in next week's work.

2. Lead the content review of "Pray in Faith." Use items 5-11. Do not use items that pertain to materials members will study next week.

3. Preview next week's assignments. Assign members days 4 and 5 in the material. During this preview time, focus on the assignments they will be responsible for next week.

SECOND WEEK

Follow the Standard Plan for the remainder of the group session with the exception of the following three areas.

1. Divide the group in half. Ask members to share in their groups reports on adding to their Relational-Witnessing Chart names of unsaved persons they know. Ask members to pray short prayers for the individuals that fellow group members have mentioned.

2. Lead the content review of "Pray in Faith." Spend about three minutes reviewing what members learned during the first week of the study. Ask volunteers to summarize important points from last week's study. Then move on to items 12-16.

3. Preview next week's assignments. Assign members days 1–3 in the study "Look to Jesus." Members are to complete only assignments that pertain to the material they study this week.

One-to-One Plan

PART 1
Follow instructions for the Standard Plan. Help your partner with any problems he or she has with the Spiritual Armor presentation. Assist the person in learning how to pray in faith.

PART 2
Follow instructions for the Standard Plan. Help your partner understand how to compile a personal prayer journal. Show him or her your journal and explain how it is useful to you.

GROUP SESSION 5

Look to Jesus

> **Session Goals**
> By the end of the session, members will be able to demonstrate their progress toward *MasterLife* goals by ...
> - completing assignments for week 5;
> - stating the difference between life purposes and life goals;
> - evaluating their life purposes and life goals;
> - preparing their personal prayer journals;
> - presenting the Gospel Shoes part of the Spiritual Armor;
> - interceding in prayer for others.

Standard Plan

BEFORE THE SESSION

❏ Review week 5 and read and complete the learning activities for week 6 of *MasterLife 3: The Disciple's Victory*.

❏ As you complete the material, prayerfully consider whether you are looking to Jesus as you set purposes and goals in your life.

❏ Be prepared to discuss any difficulties members are encountering in developing their personal prayer journals.

❏ Call each member of the group and encourage each person to attend.

❏ Master this week's material in the leader guide.

❏ Review the goals for this session.

❏ Check with the host or hostess to be sure he or she is ready for the group this week.

❏ Arrange the meeting place so that members can sit in a circle.

❏ Have pens or pencils and extra blank paper on hand for the session.

❏ Use "Guide to Intercession" during your personal prayer time before you use it with the group.

❏ Show God's love to someone every day this week and be prepared to share your experiences with your group.

❏ Record your life purposes, life goals, and plans if you have not done so already. Have them ready to use for illustrations.

❏ Make a poster of the basic life goals (p. 98, member book).

❏ Finalize plans for the Prayer Workshop so you can share them with group members in this week's session. If the workshop is to be held away from the church, prepare a map of the location and distribute it at the end of session 6.

❏ Make all the personal preparations for the Prayer Workshop that you have asked the group to make. Plan to spend time with God. Be sure that your own personal prayer journal is up-to-date and ready for your own prayer experience.

DURING THE SESSION

PART 1 (45/60 minutes)

Introduction (20/25 minutes)

1. Share your experience of using "Guide to Intercession" during your prayer time this week. Ask volunteers to tell about their experiences. Also ask volunteers to share names of persons for whom they have interceded in prayer, including the names on their Relational-Witnessing Charts. Encourage them to share how God has guided them and given them direction in their prayer times. After they have shared, ask group members to pray about the matters shared.

2. Pair members with persons other than their spouses to check each other's "My Walk with the Master This Week." Use any extra time to review Scriptures memorized.

"Look to Jesus" (25/35 minutes)
Choose from the following list appropriate questions and activities for your group's study. Do not feel that you have to use each question. Do not exceed the time allowance.

3. Ask a member to define *life purpose*. Ask volunteers to share the life purposes that they wrote on page 85 of the member book.

4. Ask, What does it mean to follow God wholly? Recall the account of Caleb and his life purpose. Relate Caleb's life purpose to the command found in Mark 12:30. Brainstorm, How can we tell what place God occupies in our lives? Write on the chalkboard or poster paper members' responses. (*Possible responses might include: amount of time spent in prayer, Bible study, worship; degree to which we obey God, witness, disciple others; conscious effort to please God, seek His will.*)

5. Ask a volunteer to recall the two broad life purposes from Mark 12:29-31 (*loving God and loving others*).

6. Ask a member to define *life goals*. Ask someone to explain the relationship between life goals and life purposes. Use the account of Caleb to discuss the three characteristics of worthy life goals.

7. Ask a volunteer to recall a life goal that he or she set and has now attained or is in the process of attaining. Ask the person to evaluate that goal according to the three criteria. Then ask him or her to answer the question, Was it a worthy goal that was in keeping with my life purposes? If no one volunteers, select a goal such as choosing a vocation, a marriage partner, or a place to live, and go through the process of evaluating the goal. Or use the following account.

A business executive had recently rededicated his life to God. He had determined to do God's will for his life. Not long afterward he was offered a job in another city far from his home. He was being offered a higher position, but the salary was $10,000 a year less. He was not very attracted to the job, but he had a persistent feeling that it was God's will for him to take it. Ask members how they would advise him on the basis of life purposes and life goals. (He eventually took the job and became a confidant of the president of the United States, but he never could have imagined such an outcome from the circumstances.)

8. Point out how having life purposes and specific life goals can give perspective to life. Remind members that Caleb had been promised

major undertaking—some small act like a card or phone call can be a tremendous boost to someone who is hurting.

13. Close with prayer. Thank God for the progress members have made so far. Ask God to grant them courage, wisdom, and efficient use of time in the week ahead to prepare for the Prayer Workshop. Pray that each member will have courage to be victorious in spiritual warfare.

AFTER THE SESSION

❑ Meet individually or in small groups with those who are having problems in areas such as completing the Spiritual Armor presentation or compiling their personal prayer journal.
  • Identify the problem.
  • Suggest what they can do to overcome the problem.
  • Point them in the right direction.
  • Keep them going by checking back or by assigning another person to work with them.
❑ You are approaching another crucial point in *MasterLife,* and Satan will attempt to sidetrack members before the Prayer Workshop. Remember Hebrews 10:24 and Galatians 6:1. Pray for each group member by name.
❑ Send a written announcement giving information about the Prayer Workshop. Encourage each person to be present. See the sample invitation below.

In acknowledgment of your walk with the Master
and to celebrate your completion of
MasterLife 3: The Disciple's Victory,
you are cordially invited
to attend a
Growing Disciples Workshop.
(time • date • place)

Please bring your book indicating your completed assignments
and your personal prayer journal.

❑ If the Prayer Workshop is held away from the meeting site, furnish a phone number where members could be reached in an emergency. Furnish other instructions if members are to bring a sack lunch or other items such as snacks.
❑ Call anyone who might be tempted not to attend the Prayer Workshop because of incomplete assignments. Help that person if he or she needs it.

❏ Take two members with you to minister or to witness. By now you should have taken everyone in the group with you at least once during this study.

❏ Contact the meeting site for the Prayer Workshop to confirm arrangement for food, space, and other matters as needed. Arrange for any materials you need for the workshop.

❏ Read "Before the Session" for week 6 to evaluate the amount of time you will need to prepare for your next group session. At the top of the week 6 material record when you will prepare.

❏ Begin to preview *MasterLife 4: The Disciple's Mission*. You will preview book 4 for members during the Prayer Workshop.

Split-Session Plan

FIRST WEEK

1. Follow the Standard Plan for the small-group time and for checking each other's work in "My Walk with the Master This Week." Instead of the group activity on sharing about using "Guide to Intercession," use the activity about demolishing personal spiritual strongholds. Use "Guide to Intercession" the second week since members will not use it in their weekly work until then.

2. Review the content "Look to Jesus." Discuss items 3-8 only. The remaining items pertain to material members will study next week.

3. Preview next week's assignments. Assign members days 4–5 in the material. During this preview, look only at the assignments they will be responsible for next week.

SECOND WEEK

Follow the Standard Plan for part 2 with the following adjustment. Make the adjustment regarding "Guide to Intercession" as mentioned earlier. Review the content "Look to Jesus." Spend about three minutes reviewing what members learned during the first week. Ask volunteers to summarize important points from last week's study. Then move on to items 9-12.

One-to-One Plan

Follow instructions for the Standard Plan except for the following variation. In part 2 spend adequate time helping the person finalize his or her personal prayer journal. You may want to show your partner your personal prayer journal as a model. Make certain your partner will be prepared to give his or her Spiritual Armor presentation at the end of the next session.

GROUP SESSION 6

Stand Victorious

Session Goals

By the end of this session, members will be able to demonstrate their progress toward *MasterLife* goals by ...

- sharing how they have seen group members grow during *MasterLife*;
- showing God's love to someone every day this week;
- completing assignments for week 6;
- share with someone their personal testimony or a witness presentation;
- completing memory work on the Spiritual Armor presentation;
- preparing for the Prayer Workshop.

Standard Plan

BEFORE THE SESSION

- ❑ Review week 6 of *MasterLife 3: The Disciple's Victory* and read the activities for the Prayer Workshop.
- ❑ Pray daily for each member of the *MasterLife* group. Ask God for guidance and encouragement in each member's life.
- ❑ Call members of the group to confirm their attendance at the final group session and the Prayer Workshop.
- ❑ Master this week's material in the leader guide.
- ❑ Review the goals for this session.
- ❑ Check with the host and/or hostess to be sure he or she is ready for the group this week.
- ❑ Arrange the meeting place so that members can sit in a circle.
- ❑ Make any last-minute plans necessary for the Prayer Workshop. You will want to share them with group members in this week's session. Provide an emergency number where members can be reached.
- ❑ Have pens or pencils and extra blank paper on hand for the session.

DURING THE SESSION

PART 1 (45/60 minutes)

Introduction (10/15 minutes)

1. Greet members. Ask group members to share one change they have seen in the life of the person seated to their right since beginning

MasterLife 3: The Disciple's Victory. Go around the circle until each member has answered. Encourage brief answers.

2. Pray together as a group silently. Ask each person to thank God for the progress the person to his or her left mentioned.

Verifying Assignments (10/15 minutes)

3. Ask each member to pair up with another person to check each other's assignments in "My Walk with the Master This Week."

4. Encourage members to have their assignments completely checked off by the end of this session. If a member still needs a few minutes to complete an assignment, arrange to meet with that person during a break or after the session to finish checking off his or her assignments. Or ask members to get together to check any other incomplete assignments before the workshop.

"Stand Victorious" (25/30 minutes)

Choose from the following list the appropriate questions and activities for your group's study. Do not exceed the time allowance.

5. Ask volunteers to describe a situation in which they had an opportunity to show God's love to someone this week. Ask others to identify opportunities they believe they encountered but failed to pursue.

6. Ask members to describe an area of pride in their lives that needs to be demolished. Ask them to identify what they need to do to demolish it and the spiritual weapon(s) to be used.

7. Ask for volunteers to describe specific, personal prayers they have prayed based on God's person, promises, purposes, and/or previous acts. After several have shared, repeat together this week's memory verse: Ephesians 3:20-21.

8. Ask for a volunteer to share about a time he or she prayed to God and depended on God to show him or her the way.

9. Ask for a volunteer to describe a time when he or she obeyed God even though what God told him or her did not make sense.

10. Share about a time when you tried to fight a battle on your own instead of leaning on God. Then invite group members to tell about their experiences.

11. Ask group members to share as a testimony to others an experience when they stood victoriously in spiritual warfare.

12. Close this part of the session by asking members to praise God for who He is. Say, Voice a sentence prayer for yourself. Ask God to help you find ways to strengthen your relationship with Him.

Take a stand-up break. Invite participants to help themselves to refreshments.

PART 2 (45/60 minutes)

Contact with Non-Christian Friends (10 minutes)
1. Ask volunteers to report on their experiences of sharing their personal testimonies this week. Allow time for as many to share as will before you lead in a time of prayer.

2. Pray that the group members' expressions of love to lost friends will be entry points for sharing the gospel when the time is appropriate.

The Spiritual Armor (15/20 minutes)
3. Ask members to get in pairs to check each other's presentation of the Spiritual Armor. Members should have mastered the entire presentation by now. Remind those who are not checked off on their presentation to arrange to meet with another group member during the week to present the Spiritual Armor in their own words. Ask the pair to spend any extra time in prayer for each other.

Prayer Workshop Assignments (15/20 minutes)
4. Answer questions about the Prayer Workshop. If you need to explain its purpose again, refer to "Questions and Answers About the Prayer Workshop" on page 123 in the member book. Review each question.

5. Urge members who may not yet have completed all their assignments to finish them before the Prayer Workshop. At the workshop members will be asked to share with others what they have learned.

6. Review final details for the Prayer Workshop. Invite questions. Explain transportation arrangements to the site if the workshop is held away from your regular meeting place. Distribute the telephone number where members can be reached.

Closure (5/10 minutes)
7. Close with prayer. Ask God to help members as they prepare to complete their work on *MasterLife 3: The Disciple's Victory* at the Prayer Workshop.

AFTER THE SESSION
- ❑ Immediately after the session, meet individually or in small groups with those who have not completed their work or who may be having special problems. Work closely with them so they will be prepared for the Prayer Workshop.
- ❑ Make any final arrangements needed for the Prayer Workshop.
- ❑ Read "Before the Session" for the Prayer Workshop to evaluate the amount of time you will need to prepare. At the top of the material, record when you will prepare.
- ❑ Finish previewing *MasterLife 4: The Disciple's Mission*. You will preview book 4 for members during the Prayer Workshop.

Split-Session Plan

Follow the Standard Plan, making the following adjustments.

1. During week 1 lead the content review of "Stand Victorious." Review items 5-8 only. Review items 9-12 during week 2 since they pertain to material members will study then.

2. Spend time discussing questions members might have about the Prayer Workshop. The Prayer Workshop is not designed for a split session.

One-to-One Plan

Follow the Standard Plan as you work one-to-one with your partner. Pray a prayer of thanksgiving for his or her growth in *MasterLife*.

Prayer Workshop

Note to those using the Split-Session Plan and the One-to-One Plan: The *Split-Session Plan* is not appropriate for the Prayer Workshop. The workshop should be scheduled at a time when four uninterrupted hours can be devoted to it. The Prayer Workshop works well with the *One-to-One Plan*. The Strength Rally will need to be a one-to-one relationship with the other person, following the instructions that are given to the group. Have a Strength Rally for the person you are discipling first, and then let him or her follow the same procedure for you.

Workshop Goals

By the end of this four-hour workshop, members will be able to demonstrate their progress toward *MasterLife* goals by …
- spending three hours alone in prayer;
- interceding for others;
- spontaneously reporting their prayer experiences to the group;
- asking the group to pray for them and one of their life goals and supporting others in reaching their goals;
- participating in a Strength Rally;
- examining ways they plan to seek continued growth in Christ.

BEFORE THE WORKSHOP

❑ Review the basic content of *MasterLife 4: The Disciple's Mission* so you can give an overview at the Prayer Workshop.

❑ Call each member of the group and encourage him or her to attend.

❑ Master this week's material in this leader guide.

❑ Review the goals for the Prayer Workshop.

❑ Check with the persons responsible for the meeting site to be sure they are ready for the group.

❑ Make plans for starting the study of *MasterLife 4: The Disciple's Mission*. Arrange a time, date, and place for the first meeting. Be prepared to share these plans with group members. Have books on hand at the workshop for members to purchase.

❑ Choose either to show the videotape of the MasterBuilder presentation or to make the presentation yourself. If you choose to present the material yourself, preview the way Avery Willis does it on the videotape. Then develop your own script. If you choose to show the video, secure video equipment and cue the tape before the session begins.

❑ Have pens or pencils and extra blank paper on hand for the workshop.

❑ Check on arrangements for the workshop. Make sure all members know to bring the personal prayer journal they compiled as well as additional materials that have been suggested previously.

❑ Prepare the following as a printed agenda to be distributed, or write it on a poster or chalkboard.

Today's Workshop Agenda
- Introduction (5 minutes)
- Individual Prayer Time (3 hours)
- Strength Rally (20 minutes)
- *MasterLife 4: The Disciple's Mission* (30 minutes)
- Wrap-Up (5 minutes)

❑ Pray for the workshop. Members need to have a sense of accomplishment and success at the end of this final time together in *MasterLife 3: The Disciple's Victory*. They will get this from having all their work in "My Walk with the Master This Week" checked off and by experiencing an extended time in prayer.

❑ Enlist a group member to help you guide the Strength Rally for half of your group. Give this person a copy of the procedures or review them with him or her.

❑ Determine how you will handle a meal if one will be part of the workshop. If you plan to eat before the workshop begins, encourage members to finish as soon as possible so you may begin on time. Keep the meal simple; an elaborate meal takes more time, and some members will want to clean up instead of starting their personal prayer time. If you plan to eat after the sharing time, tell members that everyone is expected to stay through the Strength Rally before they begin to prepare the food. Whatever you do about eating, everyone should spend three hours alone with God.

DURING THE WORKSHOP

Introduction (5 minutes)

1. Welcome members and tell them how pleased you are that they are at the workshop.

2. Review the schedule: three hours of individual prayer, 20 minutes for the Strength Rally, 30 minutes for an overview of *MasterLife 4: The Disciple's Mission,* and five minutes for a wrap-up.

3. Inform members of the location of their individual rooms, rest rooms, water fountain, and so on. Encourage them to go directly to the places you have assigned them without talking.

4. Remind members to make a time log of what they do. Instruct them to use the last 15 to 20 minutes of prayer time to write several conclusions.

5. Briefly review the six steps for praying in faith as a send-off to the individual prayer time.

Individual Prayer Time (3 hours)

6. As the leader you should station yourself in the main room for your prayer time in case you are needed to greet members as they return. Spend the time in prayer. Do not check on members of the group or wander around.

7. Use a prearranged signal to call members back at the end of the prayer time. Signal 10 minutes before the time is up and again at the three hour limit.

8. As members return, they likely will be excited and will want to share. Ask them to share with you and those who return early what they did and what they experienced. Assure them that any combination of activities that they did during the prayer time is acceptable. As soon as all members return, move directly to the Strength Rally.

Strength Rally (20 minutes)

9. Give the instructions for the Strength Rally.

- Members will be divided into two groups. You will lead one group; the person you have enlisted will lead the other. Assure the group that you will stay on time. Often the entire group will want to stay together. Insist they form two groups unless they agree to stay for the extra time it will require.

- Place a chair in the center of the circle. Members will take turns sitting in the chair and being the focal point of the rally.

- Each person, when he or she sits in the chair, will state one goal: a long- or short-range goal or a weekly goal. The goal should be one that this person really wants to achieve but is having difficulty reaching or anticipates having difficulty reaching. The person then remains silent and listens to what other members say.

- For the next two minutes members of the group, including the leader, will remind that person of every strength and resource the person has, large or small, for reaching his or her goal. They may suggest, if they believe the person's strength warrants it, that the goal could be greater. They are not to state any shortcomings.

- The person may respond for 30 seconds, if he or she desires, by telling whether the comments have been helpful. Members will pray conversationally around the person. They may want to place their hands on the person as they pray. These prayers should not exceed a total of two minutes, after which the leader closes the prayer.

- Each person's Strength Rally will last no more than five minutes. Then the next person will sit in the center chair, present his or her goal, and listen to the Strength Rally for him or her.

10. Each person will take a turn in the center chair until everyone has participated. The leader should also take a turn. The members benefit from understanding that everyone has problems and needs help. If others are reluctant to start, present your goal first.

11. At the conclusion of the rally, call the two groups back together.

MasterLife 4: The Disciple's Mission (30 minutes)
12. Give the MasterBuilder presentation as described on pages 123-7 of book 4; or show the videotape presentation.

13. Preview *MasterLife 4: The Disciple's Mission* by reviewing the weekly titles and giving a brief overview of the content.

14. Ask for volunteers to give personal testimonies about why they are committed to continuing their study of *MasterLife*. Help group members decide whether they will continue or take time off.

15. Distribute copies of *MasterLife 4: The Disciple's Mission* for those who know they want to continue in *MasterLife*. Make arrangements for other members who need to pray about continuing to call you with their decisions during the week. Allow these members to take the book and return it if they decide to delay their study of *MasterLife*. Assure group members that regardless of what they decide about continuing, you will be available to talk or pray with them and help them with their life in Christ.

Wrap-Up (5 minutes)
16. If some members want to stay and talk or pray, encourage them to do so. Do not go overtime unless all members agree to do so. Many members probably have other plans, need to relieve a baby-sitter, or (if the workshop is on Sunday) need to get home and make preparations to return to church.

17. Sound a note of victory and excitement about the study. Members who have completed the first three books are now in the last quarter of *MasterLife*.

18. Announce the time, date, and place of the beginning of *MasterLife 4: The Disciple's Mission*. Close with prayer.

AFTER THE WORKSHOP
- ❏ Make sure the building or meeting facility is in order before you leave. Be a servant.
- ❏ Write each member expressing appreciation for his or her participation in the study. Remind him or her that you are praying as he or she continues to apply concepts of *MasterLife 3: The Disciple's Victory* to daily life.
- ❏ Finalize your plans for beginning the study of *MasterLife 4: The Disciple's Mission*. Confirm the meeting site. Post a notice in the church on a bulletin board or in the church bulletin to announce the formation of a group studying *MasterLife 4: The Disciple's Mission*. Occasionally someone who completed book 3 earlier than your group did but who has never studied book 4 will want to join your group. This type of announcement makes such people aware of your group's availability. Be careful, though, not to exceed the maximum capacity for a *MasterLife* group.
- ❏ Assume all members of your group will continue unless they tell you otherwise. If you question whether a group member will move on to the next book, call and encourage his or her participation. If a member informs you that he or she is unable to participate now, suggest that the person may want to join another group at a later date.
- ❏ This is a good time to take stock of the leadership you provided during *MasterLife 3: The Disciple's Victory*. If you believe that a problem exists between you and one of the members, visit with this person and seek reconciliation.
- ❏ Spend time in prayer for each member.
- ❏ Take members visiting with you. Tell them you may ask them to give their personal testimonies at some time during the visit. Help them continue to improve in how they share their faith with others.
- ❏ Inform the church of the progress of the group and your expectations for them by the end of the *MasterLife* training. Ask the church staff when and where some of your members can share brief testimonies about what *MasterLife* has meant to them. Members may share their salvation testimonies. Announce to the church family that names are being accepted of persons who want to enroll in *MasterLife* and begin the earlier book studies.
- ❏ Some members may want to give testimonies to the church about what the workshop meant to them. If possible, arrange for them to share. Caution them not to appear "holier than thou" because they spent a half day in prayer. Encourage them to tell how the Lord convicted them of sins as well as how He helped them experience victory.

THE DISCIPLE'S MISSION

MasterLife

BOOK 4

"Go and make disciples of all nations,
baptizing them in the name of the Father and of the Son
and of the Holy Spirit, and teaching then to obey
everything I have commanded you. And surely I am with you always,
to the very end of the age " (Matt. 28:19-20).

God will use *The Disciple's Mission* to lead group members
to join Him in making disciples by identifying
their stages in growth and their roles in ministry.

Contents

INTRODUCTORY SESSION

On Mission with the Master

Conduct this Introductory Session before your group members study week 1 of *MasterLife 4: The Disciple's Mission* if you are leading a group that has not studied *MasterLife 3: The Disciple's Victory*. If your group is moving directly from *MasterLife 3: The Disciple's Victory*, skip the Introductory Session and move directly to Group Session 1.

You might consider conducting this session if a substantial amount of time has elapsed between *MasterLife 3: The Disciple's Victory* and beginning this study or if your group did not have sufficient time at the Prayer Workshop to preview book 4.

Session Goals

By the end of this session, members will be able to demonstrate their commitment to *MasterLife* by …
- telling at least one new bit of information about each group member;
- explaining the general concepts of MasterBuilder;
- doing the week 1 assignments.

Standard Plan

BEFORE THE SESSION

❑ Review the introduction and complete the learning activities for week 1 of *MasterLife 4: The Disciple's Mission*. At the end of this session you will preview week 1 for the members.

❑ Find a quiet time and place to pray for group members by name. Ask the Lord to give you the wisdom you need to prepare for and lead the group session.

❑ Read "During the Session" and master the material.

❑ Check with the host and/or hostess to be sure he or she is prepared for the group this week.

❑ Arrange for refreshments to be served at the break or at the beginning of the session.

❑ Arrange in a circle enough chairs for everyone attending.

❑ If members have not studied *MasterLife 1: The Disciple's Cross*, *MasterLife 2: The Disciple's Personality*, and *MasterLife 3: The Disciple's Victory* or a significant amount of time has elapsed between studies, either schedule a separate session to overview this material, invite them to stay after the session, ask a person in the group to explain it later, or provide the videotapes of the presentations for them to take home. Prepare on newsprint/poster paper diagrams of the Disciple's Cross, the Disciple's Personality, and the Spiritual Armor to reference as you highlight the presentations. Consider showing the videos that accompany this study if you have time.

❑ If members of your group were not part of the same group that studied *MasterLife 3: The Disciple's Victory*, and are not acquainted, have material for name tags for everyone you expect to attend.

❑ If a significant amount of time has elapsed between the Prayer Workshop for *MasterLife 3: The Disciple's Victory* and the beginning of *MasterLife 4: The Disciple's Mission*, prepare to present MasterBuilder to acquaint group members with it or to refresh their memories.

❑ Master the Relationship Quotient evaluation process (member book, p. 14). Work through this process with a member of your family or a close friend before you attend the session.

❑ Have pens or pencils and extra blank paper on hand for the session.

❑ Prepare a poster with the following information.

Stages of Moral Development
- Level 1—Focus: Self
  Motivation: Reward and Punishment
- Level 2—Focus: Others
  Motivation: Models and Examples
  Orderliness Through Rules
- Level 3—Focus: Principles
  Motivation: Responsibility

❑ Plan to stay within the times given for each activity. The maximum time suggested for each week is 45 to 60 minutes for each part. The Introductory Session is recommended for 35 to 50 minutes for each part. You may want to make an agenda each week with the subjects and times listed. This will guide the group and allow members to help the group stay on schedule.

❑ Be prepared to tell the group about the Spiritual-Gifts Workshop scheduled for the conclusion of the study.

Remember that allowing members to share freely is far more important than sticking legalistically to a schedule. Group members sometimes arrive at a session eager to tell about something that happened in their lives during the week related to that week's content. Be sensitive to this need, and be flexible. Allow God to work in your group. Provide opportunities for everyone to respond during the session.

DURING THE SESSION

PART 1 (35/50 minutes)

Introduction (5/10 minutes)
1. Welcome each person and point members to the refreshments. If they were not together for the study of *MasterLife 3: The Disciple's Victory*, invite each person to make a name tag. As members arrive, introduce them to the others. Let everyone visit informally until time to begin.

2. Begin promptly. Remind the group that you will begin and end each session on time. If group members want to fellowship or have additional discussions after the sessions, they may do so, but they can count on you to be prompt.

3. Ask each person to share one fact about himself or herself that group members may not know. Even if members of this group were together in the *MasterLife 3: The Disciple's Victory*, they still may not know some facts about members' lives. Lead in prayer thanking God for guiding group members to participate in *MasterLife 4: The Disciple's Mission*.

The Disciple's Cross (5 minutes)
4. If this group did not participate in *MasterLife 1: The Disciple's Cross*, briefly overview the Disciple's Cross presentation. Refer to the Disciple's Cross diagram on page 122 in *MasterLife 4: The Disciple's Mission* and to the full presentation in *MasterLife 1: The Disciple's Cross*.

5. Refer to the drawing of the Disciple's Cross on newsprint/poster paper. Say, You will have assignments in each of the six disciplines each week: spending time with the Master, living in the Word, praying in faith, fellowshipping with believers, witnessing to the world, and ministering to others.

6. Explain how the Disciple's Cross relates to the Disciple's Personality. Say, The circle in the center of the Disciple's Cross is the Disciple's Personality and represents you—your total personality, a unity. Understanding what the circle represents helps you understand why you act the way you do.

7. Invite members who are not familiar with the Disciple's Cross to stay after the session for you or a person in the group who was part of a *MasterLife 1: The Disciple's Cross* to give the full presentation. Or loan them the videotape that features the presentation of the Disciple's Cross.

The Disciple's Personality (5 minutes)

8. If this group did not participate in *MasterLife 2: The Disciple's Personality*, briefly refer to the Disciple's Personality. Point members to the Disciple's Personality presentation in *MasterLife 2: The Disciple's Personality* and the drawing you prepared before the session as a point of reference. Do not explain it in detail.

9. Invite members who are not familiar with the Disciple's Personality to stay after the session for you or a person in the group who was part of *MasterLife 2: The Disciple's Personality* to give the full presentation. Or loan them the videotape that features the presentation of the Disciple's Personality.

The Spiritual Armor (5 minutes)

10. If this group did not participate in *MasterLife 3: The Disciple's Victory*, briefly refer to the Spiritual Armor presentation. Point them to the full presentation in book 3.

11. Explain how the Disciple's Personality relates to the Spiritual Armor. Say, The Disciple's Personality prepares you for the war against the world, the flesh, and the devil as you understand how the Holy Spirit works in you to build a Christlike character and helps give you an inner victory. This inner victory prepares you for the outer victory you learned how to attain in *MasterLife 3: The Disciple's Victory*. The defensive weapons of the Spiritual Armor are to protect you, and the offensive weapons are to lead you forward. The presentation of the Spiritual Armor focuses on the vertical bar of the cross—the Word and prayer—as the way to victory.

12. Invite members not familiar with the Spiritual Armor to stay after the session for you or a person in the group who was part of *MasterLife 3: The Disciple's Victory* to give the full presentation. Or loan them the videotape that features the presentation of the Spiritual Armor.

MasterBuilder (15/25 minutes)

13. Say, Up to this point you have mainly focused on the vertical relationship with God. *MasterLife 4: The Disciple's Mission* completes the horizontal bar of the Disciple's Cross as you focus on your relationships with others and the pathway to spiritual growth. MasterBuilder will complete the picture of what is meant by the term *make disciples*.

14. Give the MasterBuilder presentation (member book, p. 123). Do not draw the illustration. Explain that MasterBuilder will be learned a section at a time over a six-week period.

Take a stand-up break. Invite participants to help themselves to refreshments.

PART 2 (35/50 minutes)

Prayer Time (5 minutes)

1. Ask members to pair with another person, preferably not their spouse. Invite members to share with the other person concerns they have in their lives. Invite them to pray for each other's needs.

The Disciple's Victory (5 minutes)

2. If this group did not participate in *MasterLife 3: The Disciple's Victory* and therefore did not attend the Prayer Workshop or if considerable time has elapsed between the conclusion of the workshop and the start of this course, you may want to spend more time on the overview and course goals. Preview by reviewing the weekly titles and giving a brief overview of the content of *MasterLife 4: The Disciple's Mission*. Distribute copies of the book to group members.

Stages of Moral Development (10 minutes)

3. Explain the poster "Stages of Moral Development" that you made, using the following material.
- Level 1 examples: "I will do this to get a certain result or to prevent an unwanted result."
- Level 2 example: "I will do this because I think Jesus would do it or because my church or organization says so."
- Level 3 example: "I will do this because I know it is right."
- Say, Social scientists identify three basic levels of moral development that explain the sources of our motivation. Everyone begins at the first level, and about 60 percent of the people remain there. They are concerned about themselves and respond to the rewards and punishments offered in their environment.
- Say, About 40 percent of the people will grow to level 2. They are influenced by people they admire and want to please. Later they are attracted to orderly rules and systems that offer consistent ways of defending right and wrong.
- Say, Only 10 to 20 percent of the total population grow to level 3. They have internalized the principles until they have become a part of their personalities. They do the right things because they are consistent with their beliefs and values. They can tell you why if you ask, but do not depend on the external influence of persons or environment.
- Say, *MasterLife 1: The Disciple's Cross* began with level 1, at which you were primarily concerned about yourself and what was in it for you. It moved you toward responding to the example of Christ and a consistent lifestyle (level 2). To some, this seemed like child's play (and it may have been for them). But most of us needed the discipline of following instructions before we internalized the principles. For example, at first you did many of the assignments because *MasterLife* or the leader instructed you to, and you were concerned

about what would happen if you did not do them. Sometimes you completed the assignments because of what members of the group would think if you did not do them. Then you moved to level 2 and completed the assignments because you understood why and/or were motivated by the example of others.

- Say, Now you are moving to level 3, at which you are doing things because you believe in the principle. For example, you should have a quiet time every day because it is consistent with the life you are living in Christ rather than because the leader asked you to or because the group is checking. The lasting benefit of *MasterLife* will be what you do after the course is completed. You will live a certain way because teachings have been internalized and you believe a particular behavior is right.
- Say, Some people never reach level 3. The goal of *MasterLife* is that all group members will move closer to level 3 maturity. In level 2 we are influenced by external motivation. In level 3 we have internalized the principles and do things because of inner motivation.

4. This explanation may lead to discussion. If it does, you may need to continue the discussion rather than follow the session plan.

"Dimensions of Discipleship" (5/15 minutes)

5. Say, Discipleship is a life-changing experience. Discipleship reaches into and affects every area of a person's life. The purpose of the Bible study that follows is to help you identify the different dimensions of discipleship and consider how discipleship will affect those dimensions in your life and in the lives of others.

6. Ask members to turn to the Bible-study worksheet on page 7 in the member book. Use the following procedure to lead members to complete the statements about the different dimensions of discipleship. Ask different people to read the verse for the first statement using a variety of translations if possible. Then ask members to state how they would fill in the blank in the first statement. After brief discussion, ask members to write their answers on their worksheets if they have not done so already. The following information suggests how each statement could be completed and gives comments you may want to make.

- Verse 1: One *aim* of discipleship is that you be strengthened in Christ's grace.
- Verse 2: Part of the *mission* of discipleship is multiplying disciples, reproducing disciples, teaching others who in turn can teach others.
- Verse 3: Part of the *commitment* of discipleship is to endure hardships. Emphasize the need to be disciplined regardless of the hardships.
- Verse 4: The *focus* of discipleship is on pleasing Christ; pleasing the One who called us.

- Verse 5: The *discipline* of discipleship is to follow the rules; be obedient.
- Verse 7: The *teacher* in discipleship is the Lord.
- Verse 8: The *foundation* of discipleship is that Christ lives, was raised from the dead.
- Verse 9: The *potency* of discipleship is the unbound, unhindered Word of God; the living Word. Emphasize that when the Word has been unleashed in their lives, it makes a potent difference.
- Verse 10: The *fruit* and ultimate reason for discipleship is that the elect may be saved, the salvation of the lost.
- Verse 15: The *challenge* of discipleship is to be an approved worker, not ashamed but able to interpret the Word of God correctly.
- Verses 20-21: The *secret* of individual usefulness in discipleship is inner purification; it is impossible to be outwardly prepared if one is not inwardly pure.
- Verse 21: The *finished product* of discipleship is a cleansed vessel of the Lord, fit for the Master to use, and prepared to do every good work.
- Verses 24-25a: The *essential nature* of discipleship is servanthood—to be gentle, ready to reach, patient, meek, and instructing those who oppose themselves. Emphasize that discipleship that does not have a servant heart is not biblical discipleship.
- Verses 25b-26: Part of the *ministry* of discipleship is the ministry of restoration. This includes both winning the lost and reclaiming Christians who have lost their effectiveness.

Lead members to share which verses spoke to them and why. Invite members to commit themselves to discipleship and discipling through prayer.

Relationship Quotient (15/20 minutes)
7. Explain how to use the Relationship Quotient form (member book, p. 132). Clarify the meaning of the seven headings on the form.

8. Ask members to pair up and fill out their Relationship Quotient forms. Each person should complete the form separately before the pair discusses their responses. For this exercise, husbands and wives should work together.

9. Reassemble the group. Ask volunteers to discuss the experience as time allows. Clarify any misunderstandings about how to use the Relationship Quotient form.

10. Suggest to couples, After you return home, continue to discuss why you ranked each other as you did. Over the next few weeks you will receive more help for improving relationships. Do the Relationship Quotient evaluation with one other member of your family or with a friend this week.

Week 1 Assignments and Closure (5 minutes)

11. Ask members to look at "My Walk with the Master This Week" for week 1 on page 9 of *MasterLife 4: The Disciple's Mission* and preview the specific assignments. Say, It will be important for you to complete each assignment because it will provide an opportunity to learn by experience. A part of *MasterLife* is an accountability process by which we check each other's learning. As you complete an assignment, you will draw a vertical line through the diamond that precedes the assignment. A fellow member verifying your work during the group session will draw a horizontal line though the diamond to form a cross.

12. Preview the content of week 1. Ask members to complete the activities in "Righting Wrong Relationships" before Group Session 1 of *MasterLife 4: The Disciple's Mission.*

13. Urge members to select and pray with their prayer partners about specific matters. This may be the prayer partner they have had since their study of book 1, or they may choose someone new.

14. Invite members to begin visiting their neighbors. Explain how such a contact may lead to a time when they can share the gospel.

15. Direct members to the Personal-Assessment Worksheet (member book, p. 26). Explain that the activity will help them assess their strengths and weaknesses as disciplers by using the MasterBuilder concepts.

16. Announce the time and place for the next session. Stand and join hands in a prayer of dismissal. Ask members to voice a one-sentence prayer for the person seated to their left, especially as they begin visiting neighbors who may not know Christ.

17. Express gratitude for each member, and ask them to pray for you as you seek to lead them in the days ahead.

AFTER THE SESSION
❑ Specifically pray for each member.
❑ Call group members and encourage them in the study of the first week's material. Answer questions they may have, and thank each group member for his or her commitment to the study.
❑ If any persons express doubt about permanently joining the *MasterLife* group, consider others to take their place. Ask anyone new joining the group to complete "Righting Wrong Relationships" before the next session. They will easily be able to start week 1. New members should not join the group after Group Session 1.
❑ Use the following questions to evaluate your leadership.

- Was I thoroughly prepared?
- Was my presentation clear?
- Did I follow the leader guide?
- Did I provide positive leadership?
- Was I a servant leader?
- Did I create a group environment?
- Did I help members communicate with each other?
- Did members understand the purpose of the study?
- Was I enthusiastic about how God will use *MasterLife* in members' lives and our church?

❏ Read "Before the Session" for the first group session to evaluate the amount of preparation you will need. At the top of the first page of Group Session 1 material, record when you will prepare.

❏ Carefully study week 2 and do all the exercises in the member book. You will preview week 2 for members during Group Session 1.

Split-Session Plan

The Introductory Session should not be split. For groups following the Split-Session Plan, assign days 1-3 of the study "Righting Wrong Relationships" for the first week of Group Session 1 and days 4-5 of the study for the second week.

One-to-One Plan

PART 1

Follow directions for the Standard Plan during your first meeting. Use this opportunity to discover needs and to help meet them. Allow the person to interact and ask questions as you talk together rather than your monopolizing the conversation. Be a friend.

1. Follow the Standard Plan for referencing the Disciple's Cross, the Disciple's Personality, and the Spiritual Armor. Share with your partner how you have used these in your own life. You may have time to ask him or her to give the presentations if this member studied books 1, 2, and 3, or you as leader may give them. A third option is to watch the presentations on the videotapes provided for the study.

2. Follow the Standard Plan for giving an overview of the material in *MasterLife 4: The Disciple's Mission.* As you explain the levels of moral development, let the person comment on what motivates him or her. Ask, What activities do you do because of principle? For what types of activities do you still need examples and systems as support? All levels or moral development are OK. Although a person may be at a particular level of moral development, there could be values, beliefs, or practices

at another level. For example, the person may have a quiet time because of principle but still not witness or minister as a lifestyle (principle).

3. Present MasterBuilder. Say, You will not learn the presentation all at one time but will add new material each week. You will be expected to present MasterBuilder in your own words at the end of the study. Share how you have used MasterBuilder to benefit your own life.

PART 2

1. Follow the Standard Plan for explaining week 1 assignments.

2. Discuss the Relationship Quotient form. Discuss how your partner will use it with a family member. If the person is single, he or she may use it with a parent, relative, or close friend.

GROUP SESSION 1

Righting Wrong Relationships

Session Goals
By the end of this session, members will be able to demonstrate their commitment to *MasterLife* by …
- stating goals for their study of *MasterLife 4: The Disciple's Mission;*
- explaining the vertical and horizontal bars of the Disciple's Cross as they relate to the path of growth in MasterBuilder;
- praying for the neighbors whom they visited during the week;
- saying from memory Matthew 5:23-24;
- describing three reasons why relationships should be restored immediately;
- identifying six steps to take if someone offends them;
- completing the assignments for week 1.

Standard Plan

BEFORE THE SESSION
❑ Review the introduction and complete the learning activities for week 1 of *MasterLife 4: The Disciple's Mission.*
❑ Study week 2 and do all the learning activities in the member book. You will preview week 2 for the members at the end of this session.

❑ Find a quiet place and time to pray for members. Ask the Lord to give you the wisdom you need to prepare for and lead the session.

❑ Read "During the Session" and master this week's material.

❑ Review the goals for this session.

❑ Check with the host and/or hostess to be sure he or she is ready for the group this week.

❑ Have name tags ready if needed with your group.

❑ Begin visiting your neighbors (member book, p. 9) so you can share your experiences with group members as they discuss theirs.

❑ Continue to complete the Relationship Quotient form with other members of your family or close friends.

❑ Enlist a volunteer to play the role of an unsaved person when you demonstrate the Gospel in Hand illustration.

❑ Obtain the *MasterLife* video "Reconciliation" or master "How to Seek Reconciliation" (member book, p. 18) so you can explain and illustrate it. Make a list of the people in your circles of influence with whom you need to seek reconciliation. Seek to initiate reconciliation first with the one you think will be most difficult. Do this before the next session so you can share your personal experience.

❑ Arrange for refreshments to be served at the beginning of the session or at the break.

❑ Arrange chairs in a circle for everyone in the group.

❑ Have pens or pencils and extra blank paper on hand for the session.

❑ Plan to stay within the times given for each activity. The maximum time suggested is 45 or 60 minutes for each part. You may want to print an agenda with the subjects and times listed. This will guide the group and allow members to help the group stay on schedule.

❑ Order *MasterLife* pins to distribute at the workshop for those who completed all four studies. See page 7 for ordering information.

Remember that allowing members to share freely is far more important than sticking legalistically to a plan you develop for the group session. Group members sometimes arrive at a session eager to tell about something that happened in their lives during the week related to that week's content. Be sensitive to this need, and be flexible. Allow God to work in your group. Provide opportunities for everyone to respond during the session.

DURING THE SESSION

PART 1 (45/60 minutes)

Introduction (10/15 minutes)

1. Welcome each person and point members to the refreshments. Tell them you are glad they are participating in *MasterLife*. Let everyone visit informally until time to begin.

2. Begin promptly. Remind the group that you will begin and end each session on time. If group members want to fellowship or have additional discussions after the sessions, they may do so, but they can count on you to be prompt.

3. If your group members were together for *MasterLife 3: The Disciple's Victory* and therefore did not participate in the Introductory Session, give a brief overview of the material and course goals for *MasterLife 4: The Disciple's Mission*. If they participated in the Introductory Session, skip the overview.

4. Introduce any new members of the group. Ask them to give one fact that will help others remember their names. Ask group members to sign the covenant on page 8 of *MasterLife 4: The Disciple's Mission*. If members did not participate in *MasterLife 3: The Disciple's Victory* and are starting with this book, they may not know the purpose and importance of the covenant. Explain it at this time.

5. Ask each member to give a brief statement of his or her goals for this study. Call the group to prayer. Invite volunteers to say sentence prayers asking God to help group members achieve their goals.

MasterBuilder (10/15 minutes)
6. Share how you used the concepts of MasterBuilder during your quiet times the past week. Then ask two or three members to share their experiences.

7. Ask members to pray conversationally in groups of four about the experiences group members shared.

"How to Seek Reconciliation" (25-30 minutes)
8. Show the video "Reconciliation" if available. If not, explain the contents of "How to Seek Reconciliation" (member book, p. 18). Ask members to quietly let the Spirit shine His light on their hearts. Encourage them to share what God is convicting them of or to pray directly to God. Group members should support each other with prayers and encouragement to let Christ forgive them. If God moves in the group, you may need to postpone the rest of the activities in this session to allow members to get right with God and any other person(s).

9. Use the following material if you are explaining the contents of "How to Seek Reconciliation."
• Read and comment on Hebrews 12:14-15. Explain a *bitter root* and its results.
• Explain guidelines for seeking reconciliation, adding personal illustrations. Encourage members to ask questions about points they do not understand.

- Urge members to do all they can to weed out roots of bitterness in their circles of influence.
- Encourage members to seek reconciliation. Tell them that most persons respond positively if we come asking forgiveness rather than assessing blame.
- Explain how persons usually try to keep the scales balanced on shame and blame. Draw a picture similar to the illustration.

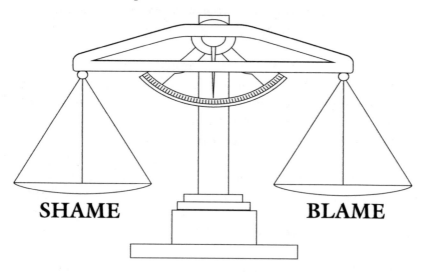

SHAME   **BLAME**

- Say, People maintain grudges by blaming others for actions or attitudes they are ashamed of or that they know they should be ashamed of. As long as they can place blame on another person, they do not have to feel shame. If they can keep shame and blame in balance, they can feel OK. When you confess something that others also feel is wrong, they will not be able to accept your confession and will continue to blame you. Therefore, they will feel shame for what they have done. They will seek to balance the scales again by:

  a. Asking your forgiveness and thereby ridding themselves of shame.
  b. Refusing to accept your confession so they can continue to blame you and keep the scales balanced. Sometimes they will blame you for something else or blame someone else (even God) for their shameful acts. However, this is the opportunity for the Holy Spirit to change shame to guilt and to convict them. They often later seek forgiveness from God and from you.
  c. Feeling shame and blaming themselves for everything. The solution is for them to experience God's forgiveness. Here is your chance to help by sharing your personal testimony of forgiveness.

10. Say, When you seek reconciliation, you may be the opening the door to a witness. However, don't jump in too quickly with the gospel presentation. The person may think your asking for forgiveness is just a manipulative tool. Waiting a few days to share your witness may give the person more time to reflect on the fact that you were sincere when you asked for forgiveness.

Take a stand-up break. Invite participants to help themselves to refreshments.

PART 2 (45/60 minutes)

"Righting Wrong Relationships" (25/30 minutes)
Choose from the following list appropriate activities for your group. Do not exceed the time allowance.

1. Ask members to recall the three reasons a wrong relationship between Christians should be immediately restored. Ask, What happens to a relationship that continues to have unresolved conflicts? Write responses on one side of a chalkboard or poster paper. (*loss of trust, bitterness, resentment, lack of intimacy, hurt feelings*)

2. Ask, What are values to be gained by restoring a wrong relationship? Write responses on the other side of the chalkboard or poster paper. (*humbles a person, thus preventing the sin of pride; draws people together; results in a clear conscience; exalts God; prevents bitterness from growing*)

3. Ask members to respond to the question, Which of these roles is the most difficult for you to carry out?
   • Asking forgiveness when you are the offender
   • Seeking reconciliation when you have been offended
   • Acting as a peacemaker

4. Lead the group in a discussion of asking forgiveness when you are the offender.
   • How should you prepare yourself for the act of asking forgiveness? (*pray, ask God's forgiveness, plan restitution*)
   • Are there some sins that should be confessed only to God? (*Yes, such as mental sin that another person is not aware of. Confession should be only as public as the sin.*)
   • What do you do if the other person refuses to forgive you? (*You are not responsible for the other person's reaction as long as you have asked for forgiveness and have been tactful and specific.*)

5. Ask, Is forgiveness a feeling to be experienced or an act of obedience to be performed? (*Feelings follow actions.*) Read 1 John 3:21-22.

6. If time permits, role-play in three to five minutes a situation in which one member asks forgiveness from another member. Let the group decide what the problem has been and how the actors are to deal with reconciliation. After the role play, discuss what happened. Offer suggestions for other ways to approach such situations.

7. Ask members to discuss their understanding of making restitution. Ask, What do you think some of the biggest barriers are to making restitution? (*embarrassment, pride, fear of retaliation*) Invite volunteers to share experiences they have had in making restitution after they have asked for forgiveness from another person.

8. Discuss the qualifications of a peacemaker and allow the group to identify situations in which a peacemaker could be helpful. Contrast the role of peacemaker with that of busybody.

9. Invite volunteers to share experiences they have had in seeking reconciliation. Pray that God will enable members to have a clear conscience in all their relationships.

The Spiritually Dead Person (5/10 minutes)
10. Review for members the Spiritually Dead part of MasterBuilder (member book, p. 124). Show them how it fits into the overall context of MasterBuilder. Remind members that they are not expected to memorize the entire presentation yet but to learn the general principles as they add elements each week.

11. Ask volunteers to discuss their progress on the Personal-Assessment Worksheets they completed in this week's work. Ask them to share the highest stage they believe they have reached in their spiritual development and a stage they believe they need to model better.

The Gospel in Hand Presentation (10/15 minutes)
12. Give the presentation to the person you have enlisted to role-play a non-Christian.

13. Explain the "Gospel in Hand" illustration (member book, p. 128).

Next Week's Assignments (5 minutes)
14. Ask members to look at "My Walk with the Master This Week" for week 2 in *MasterLife 4: The Disciple's Mission*. Preview the specific assignments. Remind them again that as they complete an assignment, they are to draw a vertical line through the diamond. A fellow member verifying their work during Group Session 2 will draw a horizontal line through the diamond to form a cross.

15. Briefly preview the content of week 2. Ask members to complete the activities in "Witnessing and Discipling Through Relationships" before the next session.

16. Call attention to the assignment that asks members to continue visiting their neighbors and discovering prayer requests. Encourage members to be open to witnessing opportunities.

17. Point out that members are also asked to continue using the Relationship Quotient form this week—with family members or close friends.

18. Note that members are asked to study "An Approach to Witnessing" during week 2. Say, This material will help you understand how to approach individuals when you want to share the Gospel in Hand presentation you are learning.

Closure (5 minutes)

19. Stand and join hands in a prayer of dismissal. Ask members to voice one-sentence prayers for the person seated to their left, especially as that person relates to spiritually dead individuals during the coming week.

20. Suggest that members encourage each other between weekly sessions. Express gratitude that you are part of the group, and request members' prayers for you as you undertake to serve them during the weeks that follow.

AFTER THE SESSION

❑ Pray daily for members as they seek to be reconciled to family, friends, and associates. One of Satan's main devices is to keep people from forgiving others. Read 2 Corinthians 2:10-11. Pray that members will feel a responsibility to forgive others and seek reconciliation.

❑ Help members who are having difficulty seeking reconciliation. Ask members privately about the progress of their efforts to seek reconciliation. Be prepared to go with them if asked to do so.

❑ Call and encourage each group member. Answer any questions the person may have. Thank each group member for his or her commitment to the group.

❑ Use the following questions to evaluate your leadership.
  • Was I thoroughly prepared?
  • Was my presentation clear?
  • Did I follow the leader guide?
  • Did I provide positive leadership?
  • Was I a servant leader?
  • Did I create a group environment?
  • Did I help members communicate with each other?
  • Did members understand the purpose of the study?
  • Was I enthusiastic about what *MasterLife* can do in members' lives and our church?

❑ Read "Before the Session" for Group Session 2 to evaluate the amount of preparation you will need. At the top of the first page of the material, record when you will prepare.

❑ Carefully study week 3 and do all the exercises in the member book. You will preview week 3 for members during Group Session 2.

Split-Session Plan

Follow the Standard Plan for parts 1 and 2 of Group Session 1 for weeks 1 and 2 respectively. In each session have members check assignments. Make adjustments for any assignments that are to be done for the second session. Assign days 1-3 of "Witnessing and Discipling Through Relationships" for the first week of session 2 and days 4-5 for the second week.

One-to-One Study Plan

PART 1

Follow instructions for the Standard Plan. You may be able to be more open and specific in a one-to-one situation than you would be in a group. Your openness and personal experience in overcoming relationship problems will be helpful. This may become a counseling session, especially if the person has held a grudge for many years.

PART 2

Follow the Standard Plan. In the role play, play the person asking forgiveness while your partner plays the offended person. Model the right way to ask forgiveness. Then reverse roles and role-play again. Discuss how each of you could have done a better job in asking forgiveness.

Discuss how much support the other person needs to maintain consistency in completing assignments. Arrange to help him or her or to check "My Walk with the Master This Week" when needed. Everyone needs support at one time or another. Be available. Offer your assistance.

GROUP SESSION 2

Witnessing and Discipling Through Relationships

Session Goals

By the end of this session, members will able to demonstrate their progress toward *MasterLife* goals by …

- reporting on experiences in using the Relationship Quotient form with a spouse or family member;
- sharing how their relationships with others have improved;
- completing week 2 assignments;
- naming ways they can reveal the Father to the people they disciple;
- drawing the Gospel in Hand to present the gospel;
- explaining the principles of witnessing for the Spiritually Dead person in MasterBuilder;
- saying from memory Romans 6:23;
- continuing to pray for group members' neighbors and their prayer requests.

Standard Plan

BEFORE THE SESSION

❑ Review week 2 and read and complete the learning activities for week 3 of *MasterLife 4: The Disciple's Mission.*

❑ Pray daily for each member of the group. Ask the Lord to give you wisdom to prepare for and lead the group session.

❑ Master this week's material in the leader guide.

❑ Review the goals for this session.

❑ Check with the host and/or hostess to be sure he or she is ready for the group this week.

❑ Arrange the meeting place so that members can sit in a circle.

❑ Have pens or pencils and extra blank paper on hand for the session.

❑ Be prepared to share about your experiences in using your Relationship Quotient form with a spouse or family member.

❑ Review "How to Seek Reconciliation" and be prepared to help members who are encountering problems in this area.

❑ Review "An Approach to Witnessing" (member book, pp. 36-8) to share highlights and lead a discussion about what members learned.

❑ Secure enough copies of *Welcome to God's Family* and *Survival Kit: Five Keys to Effective Spiritual Growth* to distribute one to each member during this group session.

❑ Review the Gospel in Hand presentation so you can explain it to members in your own words. Enlist a person to play the role of a non-Christian as you demonstrate this drawing.

❑ Begin making plans for the Spiritual-Gifts Workshop that follows *MasterLife 4: The Disciple's Mission*. Be prepared to give suggestions about the time and place, or during this session announce to members these details if they have already been determined. A retreat setting is ideal, but meeting at church may be best for your group in terms of convenience and expense. Other workshop instructions will appear later in group-session plans.

DURING THE SESSION

PART 1 (45/60 minutes)

Introduction (15/20 minutes)
1. Greet members as they arrive. Begin on time. Be alert to any signs of progress or any problems members may be facing. Ask for special prayer requests. Open the session with prayer.

2. Ask volunteers to share the results of their efforts to improve relationships with others. Mention two possibilities for testimonies: sharing Relationship Quotient experiences with a spouse or family member and seeking reconciliation.

3. Ask members to pair with someone other than their spouses to check each other's work on "My Walk with the Master This Week." Instruct pairs to ask each other if he or she did the assignment. The persons verifying may ask to see the work. Tell them to make certain members quote memory verses correctly before that activity is marked as verified.

"Witnessing and Discipling Through Relationships"
(20/30 minutes)
4. Say, Please complete the learning activities and master the material before you attend the group session. The purpose for discussing the material in the group session is to reflect on it, explore the subject further, and apply it.

5. Ask members to discuss ways they can glorify the Father as they follow Jesus' model of glorifying the Father.

6. Invite a volunteer to quote from memory the definition of *discipleship* (see member book, p. 31).

7. Ask, Do you find it difficult to believe you can have an intimate and personal relationship with Christ? Say, Sometimes individuals struggle

with believing this in their hearts even though they know it in their heads to be true. Sometimes people relate their concept of God to an early parent who may or may not have been trusting and open.

8. Ask, Do you believe that God has sent you individuals to witness to and disciple? On what do you base this belief?

9. Ask members to discuss ways they can reveal God to people they disciple.

10. Ask members to tell of times they failed to give God credit for something they achieved for Christ with His help. Ask what they learned from the experience.

11. Invite members to describe a time when they emulated someone who lived life differently from the world's standards. Then ask them to describe a time they believe someone followed them for the same reason.

12. Give a personal illustration of a way you believe you have modeled unity for those you lead. Then ask for volunteers to give their suggestions on how to promote the type of unity Jesus taught.

13. Ask members to share reasons they believe the fields are ripe for harvest today with opportunities to spread the good news of Christ.

14. Invite volunteers to describe times when they failed to see the harvest—lost people all around who needed the gospel message.

15. Ask, How do you feel when you realize that Jesus' purpose for you is to make fruit that will last? Invite volunteers to share how they believe they are progressing in this area.

Take a stand-up break. Invite participants to help themselves to refreshments.

PART 2 (45/60 minutes)

Prayer Time (5 minutes)
1. Ask group members to pair up and share with their partner experiences visiting neighbors. Share any progress that has occurred on the request the neighbor made. Ask members to pray for each others' situations and witnessing opportunities.

Witnessing (25/35 minutes)
2. Share with group members what you considered to be the highlights of "An Approach to Witnessing" in week 2. Say, As you learn the

Gospel in Hand presentation, you will discover ways to introduce a witnessing conversation. Ask, Has anyone used the FIRE acrostic in opening a witnessing conversation? What insights have you gained from this material?

3. Give the Gospel in Hand presentation to the person you have enlisted to role-play a non-Christian. Explain how the Gospel in Hand (member book, p. 128) illustration enables members to draw the hand as they present it.

4. Ask members to get into pairs and explain to each other their understanding of the Gospel in Hand. Learning this in their own words is an effective way to explain the good news of Christ.

5. Remind members that they should be able to explain through the Spiritually Dead person part of MasterBuilder.

Welcome to God's Family (10/15 minutes)
6. Give each member the booklet *Welcome to God's Family*. Say, You should use this booklet immediately after the person accepts Christ. You will read an explanation of the booklet during week 3. Learn the basic ideas so you can explain the booklet without having to read from it.

7. Review with members the basic concepts of following up a new believer (member book, p. 61).

Next Week's Assignments (5 minutes)
8. Ask members to look at "My Walk with the Master This Week" for week 3 on page 47 in the member book.

9. Call members' attention to the assignment about being reconciled with a difficult person. Remind them that sharing the gospel with others is difficult if relationships are not right.

10. Highlight the assignment about visiting one of the non-Christians for whom they have been praying. This may present an opportunity to use the Gospel in Hand presentation.

11. Praise members for their progress and encourage them to keep up the good work. Deal with problems or questions members have.

12. Announce the time and place for the next session. Close with prayer. Ask God to help members as they visit non-Christian friends this week.

AFTER THE SESSION
❑ Evaluate the session. List activities you believe were effective. Consider ways to improve future sessions.

❏ Evaluate responses to witnessing and discipling through relationships. Talk with members you think need personal help.

❏ Look for opportunities to sincerely praise members, particularly any who may be experiencing problems. Offer your help as needed.

❏ Take one or more members visiting. Don't ask them to do anything they are not experienced doing. The purpose is for them to observe. Before each visit, tell them what you expect to find and do. After the visit, talk about what you did and did not do and why you conducted the visit as you did. By the end of the study you should have visited at least once with every member.

❏ Read "Before the Session" for Group Session 3. Evaluate the amount of preparation you will need for your next group session. At the top of the first page of the Group Session 3 material, record when you will prepare.

❏ Carefully study week 4 and do all the exercises in the member book. You will preview week 4 for members during Group Session 3.

❏ Follow up on arrangements for the Spiritual-Gifts Workshop. Enlist others to help as necessary.

Split-Session Plan

FIRST WEEK

1. Invite members to tell about experiences praying with their prayer partners. Save the introductory items until the second week since members learn about these activities during the second week.

2. Lead "Witnessing and Discipling Through Relationships." Use items 4-7 only. Items 8-15 pertain to material members will study next week.

3. Assign members days 4-5 in the study. Remind members that your group is using the Split-Session Plan. This means members will check off only those assignments that pertain to the material they have studied that week. For example, members were assigned only days 1-3 of the first week for this session. Therefore, they would not be able to check off the assignment about using the Relationship Quotient form because that assignment does not appear until day 4. The other assignments will be done the following week. During this preview time, review only the assignments they will be responsible for next week.

SECOND WEEK

1. Arrive early. Begin the session on time. Use shorter times for each activity as necessary.

2. Open the session with prayer. Ask volunteers to share results of their efforts to improve relationships with others. Mention two possibilities

for testimonies: sharing Relationship Quotient experiences with a spouse or family member and seeking reconciliation.

3. Pair members with persons other than their spouses. Each member of the pair should check the other person's "My Walk with the Master This Week." The boxes with vertical marks should be verified and marked to form a cross.

4. Review what members learned during "Witnessing and Discipling Through Relationships." Ask for a volunteer to summarize an important point from last week's study. Then move on to activities 8-15.

5. Follow instructions in the Standard Plan for *Welcome to God's Family*.

6. Preview next week's assignments. This will not take as much time to explain because of the members' experience the previous week. Assign members days 1-3 in "Establishing Spiritual Children." Members are to complete only assignments that pertain to the material for this week. Close in prayer, praying that members will continue to work to build witnessing relationships.

One-to-One Plan

PART 1
1. Follow instructions in the Standard Plan. Discuss how many relationships have been made right and how many still need to be made right. Help the person root out all bitterness so the fruit of the Spirit can grow unhindered. You may need to accompany the person if a church member will not respond to his or her attempts at reconciliation. Encourage the person to do everything possible to bring about reconciliation and help him or her understand this may not happen immediately.

2. Share opportunities you have had to witness through relationships. Share the suggestions in the material that you have found helpful. Be frank in discussing challenges you have faced as you witnessed in the course of your day-to-day activities.

3. Tell why you believe the fields are ripe for harvest today with opportunities to spread the good news of Christ. Ask the person to share his or her opinion about these opportunities.

PART 2
Follow the directions for the Standard Plan. You should have time to go more in-depth with each section than if you were in a group.

GROUP SESSION 3

Establishing Spiritual Children

Session Goals

By the end of this session, members will be able to demonstrate their progress toward *MasterLife* goals by …

- completing week 3 assignments;
- explaining the Spiritual Child part of MasterBuilder;
- demonstrating the Gospel in Hand presentation;
- describing their experiences in visiting and sharing with non-Christians;
- sharing ways they envision using *Welcome to God's Family;*
- sharing their experiences in trying to be reconciled to difficult persons;
- naming five guidelines for following up;
- describing follow-up methods used by Barnabas, Jesus, and Paul.

Standard Plan

BEFORE THE SESSION

❑ Review week 3 and read and complete the learning activities for week 4 of *MasterLife 4: The Disciple's Mission.*

❑ Call members who are having problems completing assignments to ask them how they are doing this week and to encourage them.

❑ Master this week's material in the leader guide.

❑ Review the goals for this session.

❑ Check with the host and/or hostess to be sure he or she is ready for the group this week.

❑ Arrange the meeting place so that members can sit in a circle.

❑ Have pens or pencils and extra blank paper on hand for the session.

❑ Continue to make plans for the Spiritual-Gifts Workshop.

❑ Make an effort to reconcile with someone you consider difficult. Be prepared to share about this experience with group members.

❑ Look for opportunities for encouraging a new Christian. Be prepared to share your experience with group members.

❑ If members do not appear to be keeping up with their assignments using the Standard Plan or will not be able to give the MasterBuilder presentation successfully by Group Session 6, extend week 4 assignments over the next two weeks. To do this, use the Split-Session Plan for session 4. Decide now so you can give the proper instructions for the plan you will use this week.

❑ Prepare to give five dollars to each member to use in a ministry to a needy person this week. You may give members the money yourself, knowing that you are giving to the Lord or the church may agree to fund this activity. Members will feel a keen responsibility if they know you have given them the money, and it will help them use the money wisely. Become familiar with "Guide to Financial Partnership with God" in week 4 so you can explain it to the group in this session.

❑ Make copies of the Discipleship Inventory scoring sheet (pp. 67-70 in this guide) for each member. You will distribute these at the end of Group Session 3 for members to use during their week 4 work. Make sure you take the Discipleship Inventory again so you can share your progress with the group.

DURING THE SESSION

PART 1 (45/60 minutes)

Introduction (20/30 minutes)

1. Begin the session on time even if all members are not present. Encourage members to share progress on overcoming problems they have experienced in their work.

2. Ask members for reports on experiences they have had in encouraging new Christians. Tell your experience first then invite others to share.

3. Invite volunteers to share experiences in continuing to pray for neighbors' prayer requests. Instruct members to pray about the experiences and requests mentioned.

4. Ask group members to pair up and quote 1 Peter 2:2-3 to each other. Encourage husbands and wives not to pair up. As members work in pairs, instruct them to verify each other's "My Walk with the Master This Week." Remind them to make the horizontal mark in the diamonds after verifying completed work. Encourage pairs to share their strong and weak points in completing the assignments.

"Establishing Spiritual Children" (25/30 minutes)

Choose those activities from the following list that are appropriate for your group. Do not exceed the time allowance.

5. Ask members to share ways they can help nurture a spiritual child. Ask them to describe ways others nurtured them when they were new Christians.

6. Invite volunteers to describe what they think it means in 1 Peter 2:2-3 to "grow up in your salvation."

7. Ask members to discuss "Nurturing a New Believer" (member book, p. 49). Ask for volunteers to share ideas most helpful to them and to share ways they can envision using *Welcome to God's Family* with new believers.

8. Ask, What can we learn from Barnabas's role as an encourager of Paul as a new Christian?

9. Ask, Have any of you ever had experiences such as Helen, Walter, and Steve had as encouragers of the new Christians in the case studies on pages 54-55 of the member book? If so, what did you do in such instances?

10. Ask members to describe what they learned from studying how Jesus discipled Peter. Invite a volunteer to share about a time when someone's rebuke of them helped them mature in the Christian life.

11. Ask members to tell how they imagine these ways Paul followed-up with new Christians were effective:
   • personal example
   • personal letters
   • brotherly or parental love

12. Invite volunteers to tell the five guidelines for following up a new believer that they learned in day 5.

13. Ask, What are some things you've learned in *MasterLife* that you think might be helpful for a new Christian to know? (*having a quiet time, memorizing Scripture, taking notes from a sermon, fellowshipping with believers*)

14. Ask, What has kept you going in the process of becoming a disciplined disciple?

15. Invite volunteers to share ways they experienced great enthusiasm for sharing their faith with others when they were new Christians.

16. Ask members to share their responses to these statements in day 5: "God made us to reproduce our faith. It is normal and natural for a Christian to want to reproduce."

17. Close in prayer, asking God to help group members disciple new Christians.

Take a stand-up break. Invite participants to help themselves to refreshments.

PART 2 (45/60 minutes)

Training in Discipleship (30/40 minutes)
1. Ask group members to pair up and share their experiences in trying to be reconciled with difficult persons. Invite members to pray for each other's situations and that witnessing opportunities and healing of relationships will occur.

2. Practice the Gospel in Hand presentation. Say, Today you will demonstrate in pairs how to draw the hand as you learned during week 3. The goal is to practice this until you know it by heart and can use it with a lost person.

3. Give an amount of money (five dollars suggested) to each member. Tell the members that the money is the Master's and He is trusting them to use it for Him to help someone this week. Call attention to "Guide to Financial Partnership with God" (member book, p. 72) that members will read next week. Explain that they will relate the material to the money they give away.

4. Remind members that they should be able to explain through the Spiritual Child part of MasterBuilder.

Next Week's Assignments (5 minutes)
5. Ask members to look at "My Walk with the Master This Week" for week 4 and preview specific assignments. Make sure they understand how to complete each assignment.

6. Briefly preview the content of week 4. Ask members to complete "Maturing as a Disciple" before session 4.

7. Call attention to the assignment about spending meaningful time with a family member. This is another opportunity to work on building healthy relationships. Members may choose a friend for this activity if they do not live with or near family members.

8. Note for members "How to Lead to Commitment" (member book, pp. 79-81). Say, This will help you learn how to guide individuals to make decisions for Christ. Explain this material to someone else in your own words in an effort to memorize concepts.

9. Tell members about the upcoming Spiritual-Gifts Workshop. Share details you may have acquired during the week.

10. Point members to the Discipleship Inventory (member book, p. 133) and distribute copies of the scoring sheet. Say, You will take the inventory during week 4. This is the same inventory you took during

MasterLife 1: The Disciple's Cross. You will compare your scores. If you did not participate in *MasterLife 1: The Disciple's Cross*, take the inventory and determine in which areas you need to grow as a disciple. We will discuss this in next week's session.

11. Remember that week 4 is a logical time to use the Split-Session Plan because of the amount of material and concepts dealt with. If used, instruct members to do only the assignments that pertain to the material covered in the first of the two sessions.

12. Announce the time and place for the next session. Stand and join hands in a prayer of dismissal. Ask members to voice one-sentence prayers for the person on their right. Say, Ask God to help this member continue to grow in his or her relationship with God.

AFTER THE SESSION

❑ Meet individually or in small groups with members who seem to be having problems with seeking reconciliation in difficult circumstances. Pray with them about their problems

❑ Encourage any members who may be lagging behind in their assignments. Help them with any problems. If necessary, enlist another member to work with them.

❑ Take one or more members visiting. Give them opportunities to use the witness and ministry skills they are developing. Do not push them too fast, but give them opportunity to do all they can at this point.

❑ Pray for members. This is the best support you can give them as they seek to live the life of a good disciple.

❑ Read "Before the Session" for Group Session 4 to evaluate the amount of time you will need to prepare for the next group session. Record at the top of the first page of the Group Session 4 material when you will prepare.

❑ Carefully study week 5 and do all the exercises in the member book. You will preview week 5 for members during Group Session 4.

❑ Continue to make arrangements for the Spiritual-Gifts Workshop.

Split-Session Plan

FIRST WEEK

1. Ask members for reports on their experiences in encouraging new Christians. Tell your experiences. Ask volunteers to share experiences in continuing to pray for neighbors' prayer requests. Pray, asking for volunteers to pray short prayers about the experiences and requests mentioned.

2. Ask members to work in pairs to check off each other's "My Walk with the Master This Week."

3. Lead the study "Establishing Spiritual Children." Review items 5-11 only. Items 12-17 pertain to material members will study next week.

4. Preview next week's assignments. Assign members days 4-5 in the study. During this preview time, review only the assignments they will be responsible for next week.

SECOND WEEK

1. Ask for volunteers to share their experiences in visiting non-Christians and in trying to be reconciled with difficult people. Spend time in prayer, asking for volunteers to pray specific prayers about situations discussed.

2. Ask members to work in pairs to check off each other's "My Walk with the Master This Week." They should place horizontal marks in the diamond boxes after verifying completed work.

3. Lead the study "Establishing Spiritual Children." Spend three minutes reviewing what members learned during the first week. Ask volunteers to summarize important points from last week's study. Then move to questions 12-17.

4. Preview next week's assignments. Follow the instructions in the Standard Plan about previewing assignments. Assign members days 1–3 in "Maturing as a Disciple." Members are to complete only assignments that pertain to the material they study this week. Close in prayer.

One-to-One Plan

PART 1

Follow instructions for the Standard Plan. Since you are relating to only one person, you can focus help on specific needs. For example, ask if the person needs any special help with the Gospel in Hand presentation.

PART 2

Follow instructions for the Standard Plan. Give individual time to help this person learn the concepts of MasterBuilder so he or she can present it in his or her own words. The goal is not to memorize a set of facts but to make this illustration real and personal so that the member can share from the heart about the path of spiritual growth.

GROUP SESSION 4

Maturing as a Disciple

Session Goals

By the end of this session, members will be able to demonstrate their progress toward *MasterLife* goals by …

- listing and applying five principles Jesus used to develop disciples;
- completing week 4 assignments;
- explaining the Spiritual Disciple part of MasterBuilder;
- saying from memory Luke 6:40;
- recalling how they spent meaningful time with family members;
- reporting on their use of the money entrusted to them to help someone;
- making a contract to partner with God in the use of possessions.

Standard Plan

BEFORE THE SESSION

- ❑ Review week 4 and read and complete the learning activities for week 5 of *MasterLife 4: The Disciple's Mission.*
- ❑ Pray for members of your group. Some may become discouraged as the amount of work to accomplish before a session increases. Ask God for guidance and encouragement in each member's life.
- ❑ Master this week's material in the leader guide.
- ❑ Review the goals for this session.
- ❑ Check with the host and/or hostess to be sure he or she is prepared for the group this week.
- ❑ Arrange the meeting place so that members can sit in a circle.
- ❑ Have pens or pencils and extra blank paper on hand for the session.
- ❑ Review the memory verses to date to be sure that you know them.
- ❑ Review "How to Lead to Commitment" (member book, pp. 79–81). Be ready to share with group members about a time you used it in witnessing.
- ❑ Review "How to Prepare a Message Based on a Bible Study" (member book, pp. 101-3) so you can highlight it for members in preparation for week 5.
- ❑ Be prepared to explain "How to Conduct Family Worship" (member book, p. 97).
- ❑ Take the Discipleship Inventory so you can share your personal progress with the group.
- ❑ Survey the location selected for the Spiritual-Gifts Workshop. Determine which rooms the group will use.

DURING THE SESSION

PART 1 (45/60 minutes)

Introduction (25/30 minutes)
1. Arrive early and greet members as they arrive. Be alert and available to discuss any questions they may have. Begin on time and with prayer.

2. Pair members with persons other than their spouses to check each other's "My Walk with the Master This Week." Members can use extra time to review memory verses learned so far.

3. Share with the group your experiences of taking the Discipleship Inventory. Tell about progress you have made and areas where you still need to grow. Ask for members to share their testimonies about taking the inventory again and comparing it to their scores in *MasterLife 1: The Disciple's Cross* (or taking it for the first time, if they did not study book 1). Ask, What did the inventory reveal about ways you need to grow as a disciple of Christ? For example, how are you doing in the area of taking time for prayer and meditation compared to the previous time you took the inventory? How readily do you forgive others or share the gospel with others compared to the previous time? Ask volunteers to share one specific behavior, attitude, action, or characteristic in which they would like to grow.

"Maturing as a Disciple" (15/20 minutes)
Choose from the following appropriate activities for your group. Do not feel that you have to use each activity. Do not exceed the time allowance.

4. Ask for a volunteer to recall the three types of illustrations of growth Paul used to describe a mature disciple (*biological, botanical, construction*).

5. Ask a volunteer to identify reasons people should give. (*Because Satan has blinded unbelievers; because of our experience of God's grace in salvation.*)

6. Read 2 Corinthians 8:8-9. Ask, How much did Christ give? How does recalling that sacrifice make you feel?

7. Read 2 Corinthians 9:6-7. Ask for testimonies from members about a time when they believe they reaped as generously as they sowed.

8. Invite members to tell about a time when they gave with such a cheerful heart that they gave hilariously.

9. Ask members to recall some things that 2 Corinthians 9:8-15 says happen when you give (see member book, p. 71).

10. Challenge a member to recall the five principles Jesus used to develop disciples and the disciples' response to these principles.

11. Ask, Would someone volunteer to describe a time when someone modeled a particular trait you desired to acquire? How did you set out to acquire that trait?

12. Invite a volunteer to tell about a time when he or she coached someone and had to let that person learn on his or her own rather than giving directions every step of the way.

13. Ask members to describe ways the church commissioned Barnabas and Saul and ways Jesus commissioned Peter (member book, p. 82).

14. Ask, Why is it necessary for a person to feel that he or she is commissioned in order to begin a ministry? (*Commissioning gives people a sense of validation. They are aware that someone is standing on the sidelines cheering and praying for them.*)

15. Read Luke 6:40. Ask, How does Luke 6:40 speak to you personally in your role as disciple maker?

16. Lead the group in prayer for guidance as members learn to be disciple makers.

Guide to Financial Partnership with God (10/15 minutes)
17. Call for reports on how members used the money you gave them last week. When they have given their reports, ask what lessons they learned.

18. Relate the lessons members learned through the assignment of the use of money to the larger context of being stewards of everything God entrusts to them. Refer to the parable of the talents (Matt. 25:14-30; a talent was a sum of money worth about one thousand dollars).

19. Instruct members to turn to "Guide to Financial Partnership with God" on page 72. Review step 1 by reading each principle. Ask members to write their initials in front of principles they accept, if they have not done so already. If anyone questions a principle, read the Scriptures given. Move through the material, taking turns reading the principles and having members initial the ones they accept. When you get to step 5, suggest that members prayerfully consider renewing or restoring their partnership with God.

20. Be alert to issues that surface that need follow up. You may need to plan additional studies on stewardship after *MasterLife*. You might want to provide printed resources for those who desire further study. Do not ask to see members' signed commitments because they are between them and God.

21. Close in prayer, asking the Father to help members in their partnership with Him.

Take a stand-up break. Invite participants to help themselves to refreshments.

PART 2 (45/60 minutes)

Prayer Time (5/10 minutes)
1. Call the group together for prayer. Invite volunteers to tell about opportunities to use the Gospel in Hand presentation. Ask if anyone has witnessed or had an occasion to use the principles learned in "How to Lead to Commitment" (member book, p. 79). Share your experiences. Invite members to pray short prayers related to the experiences mentioned.

MasterBuilder(10/15 minutes)
2. Pair members with someone other than a spouse. Ask each pair to present the MasterBuilder presentation, up through the Spiritual Disciple, to each other. Members are not expected to memorize the presentation but to give it in their own words. If both members do not have time to present it this week, let the member who did not share go first in next week.

How to Prepare a Message Based on a Bible Study (10 minutes)
3. Ask, Have you noticed it is often difficult to communicate to others what you have discovered or felt in a personal Bible study? If others are studying with you, you are learning together. When you try to tell someone in a devotional, a sermon, or a speech what you have learned, it is difficult. Explain why it is necessary to use a different procedure. (See "How to Prepare a Message Based on a Bible Study," p. 101.)

4. Call attention to the week 5 assignment to prepare a message on a Sunday School lesson, a devotional, or a sermon. The members need write only the key ideas for a message on a separate sheet of paper, using an already-completed Bible study or the one they did this week.

How to Conduct Family Worship (10/15 minutes)
5. Ask, Why should Christians worship God at home? After several have responded, ask someone to read Deuteronomy 6:6-9. Say, The primary

reason Christians should worship God in the home is to be obedient to God's command.

6. Invite members to suggest other reasons why Christians should engage in family worship. Encourage members who have family worship to share their testimonies. Share your own testimony of what family worship means to your home.

7. Ask, What is needed to begin family worship in the home? After discussion, point out that the only essential ingredient is a desire to be obedient to God and a willingness to follow the leadership of the Holy Spirit.

8. Call attention to the week 5 assignment to conduct family worship with family members using "How to Conduct Family Worship." If members live alone, suggest that they keep this material for future reference in case they ever live in a family setting. If they have roommates or friends who live in the same neighborhood, they may want to have a family worship time together. If this is not practical, they should count their quiet time as family worship.

9. Say, Families may expect many obstacles and hindrances to worship in the home, and the results are sometimes disappointing. Let's pray that God will help all of us be faithful to our commitment to honor Him through worship in our homes.

Next Week's Assignments (10 minutes)
10. Ask members to look at "My Walk with the Master This Week" for week 5 on page 84 of the member book and preview the specific assignments. Make sure the members understand how to complete each assignment.

11. Briefly preview the content of week 5. Ask members to complete "Training Disciples" before Group Session 5.

12. Briefly review the principles of training disciples in MasterBuilder. Remind members that they do not need to memorize this material but should learn the principles so they can tell them in their own words.

13. Tell members they will be asked in this week's work to share their faith with a non-Christian. Remind them to take along a friend who does not witness much and who can benefit from hearing the member's testimony.

14. Remind members to begin praying that God will show them the ministry He wants them to have. Explain that more attention will be focused on this in week 6 and at the Spiritual-Gifts Workshop.

15. Announce the time and place for next week's session. Announce any additional details about the Spiritual-Gifts Workshop.

16. Remind members of the importance of having each item checked off on "My Walk with the Master" each week as soon as possible to keep these activities from accumulating at the end of the study. Offer individual help after the session if needed.

17. Close the session by dividing into groups of four or five for conversational prayer for members' needs.

AFTER THE SESSION
❑ Use the following questions to evaluate group life.
- Do members care for one another? Do they trust one another? Are they becoming more open with one another?
- Are there blocks in communication?
- Are spouses relating well as group members?
- Are members responding well to my leadership?
- Is the group becoming cliquish? Do I need to encourage members to keep reaching out?
- Do some members show undesirable attitudes toward other members? Should I take them visiting together and/or pair them up more often?
- Are members helping disciple each other?
- Do they see me as a growing disciple who is also learning from them?
❑ Continue to invite members to go visiting with you. Consider taking them to an unusual ministry spot such as a bar, street corner, jail, or nursing home.
❑ Call or see all members of the group this week to encourage or challenge them. See if anyone needs help completing assignments. Encourage members to have family worship regularly.
❑ Pray for members. Remember their prayer requests.
❑ Read "Before the Session" for Group Session 5 to evaluate the amount of time you will need to prepare for your next session. At the beginning of Group Session 5, record when you will prepare.
❑ Carefully study week 6 and do all the exercises in the member book. You will preview week 6 for members during session 5.

Split-Session Plan

FIRST WEEK
1. Follow the Standard Plan for checking each other's work in "My Walk with the Master This Week," the discussions about the Discipleship Inventory and "Guide to Financial Partnership with God," and using the five-dollar gift.

2. Lead the content review of "Maturing as a Disciple." Review items 4-11 only. Items 12-16 pertain to materials members will study next week.

3. Preview next week's assignments. Assign members days 4-5 in the study. Preview only the assignments that they will be responsible for next week.

SECOND WEEK

1. Follow the Standard Plan for part 2. Spend about three minutes reviewing what members learned during the first week of study on "Maturing as a Disciple." Ask volunteers to summarize important points from last week's study. Then move on to questions 12-16.

2. Preview next week's assignments using instruction in the Standard Plan. Assign members days 1–3 in the study "Ministering as Colaborers." Members are to complete only assignments that pertain to the material they study this week.

One-to-One Plan

PART 1
Follow instructions for the Standard Plan. Help the person with "Guide to Financial Partnership with God." Share your experiences of using your five dollars and give the person plenty of time to share his or her experiences.

PART 2
Follow instructions for the Standard Plan. Help the person understand what is involved in conducting family worship and in preparing a message from a Bible study. Explain how these practices have been meaningful to you.

GROUP SESSION 5

Training Disciples

Session Goals

By the end of this session, members will be able to demonstrate their progress toward *MasterLife* goals by ...

- completing week 5 assignments;
- reporting on ministry to their families through family worship;
- praying for the non-Christian friends of others;
- reporting on preparing a message outline of a Sunday School lesson, a devotional, or a sermon;
- listing the principles of training disciples in MasterBuilder;
- identifying the three things a person can do to become a multiplying discipler.

Standard Plan

BEFORE THE SESSION

❏ Review week 5 and read and complete the learning activities for week 6 of *MasterLife 4: The Disciple's Mission.*

❏ Be prepared to discuss any difficulties members are encountering in conducting family worship.

❏ Call members and encourage them to attend the group session.

❏ Master this week's material in the leader guide.

❏ Review the goals for this session.

❏ Check with the host and/or hostess to be sure he or she is prepared for the group this week.

❏ Arrange the meeting place so that members can sit in a circle.

❏ Share your faith with a non-Christian and be prepared to share your experience with the group.

❏ Study "An Adventure in Ministry" (member book, p. 115–16).

❏ Finalize plans for the Spiritual-Gifts Workshop so you can share them in this week's session. If the workshop is to be held away from the church, prepare a map and distribute at the end of Group Session 6.

❏ Have pens or pencils and extra blank paper on hand for the session.

DURING THE SESSION

PART 1 (45/60 minutes)

Introduction (20/25 minutes)

1. Tell your experience of sharing your faith with a non-Christian. If you took a friend with you as you witnessed, explain how you believe this

person benefited. Ask volunteers to tell about their experiences. Invite them to share the names of persons to whom they witnessed. Ask group members to pray by name for the persons mentioned and for the experiences reported. If the persons witnessed to did not accept Christ, ask members to continue praying that the individuals would eventually make this important decision.

2. Pair members with persons other than their spouses to check each other's "My Walk with the Master This Week." Use any extra time to review Scriptures memorized.

"Training Disciples" (25/35 minutes)
Choose from the following list appropriate questions and activities those best suited for your group's study. Do not feel that you have to use each question. Do not exceed the time allowance.

3. Ask, What is the only command in the Great Commission, Matthew 28:19-20? (*"Make disciples." Going, baptizing, and teaching are parts of that command.*)

4. Discuss the reasons Scriptures say we should train others to be disciples (member book, p. 85).

5. Say, Share an experience in which you became a better disciple while preparing to teach Sunday School, lead discipleship training, or serve in another capacity.

6. Ask a volunteer to identify three things a person can do to become a multiplying discipler based on 2 Timothy 2:1-7 (member book, p. 86).

7. Invite members to share about the persons they identified as good models (member book, p. 87).

8. Ask group members to share ideas about why a disciple needs to have a heart that truly belongs to the Father. Use this week's memory verse, 2 Chronicles 16:9, as the basis of your discussion.

9. Ask, How did Jesus disciple persons, based on what you learned in John (member book, p. 88)?

10. Invite volunteers to share how the fellowship of believers supports them personally in their task of disciple making. Then ask, How did you pledge to support someone in our church (member book, p. 90)?

11. Ask members to tell the group names of persons God wants them to disciple (member book, p. 94). Ask them how they can encourage the disciples they select.

12. Ask, What entanglements are most likely to divert us from giving our all to Christ's battle with evil?

13. Ask, If someone asked you, "At what spiritual level are the people you are discipling?" how would you answer? What would your answer tell about what you passed on to them?

14. Ask, How can one misstep affect a person's witness or model for Christ?

15. Talk about what can happen if a disciple is asked to do too much too soon. Ask members how they believe they can know when a disciple is mature.

16. Invite volunteers to share about times they believed they were making no progress in the life of someone they were discipling. Ask them to share how they dealt with these frustrations.

17. Call the group to prayer. Ask God to help these disciple makers endure hardship and persevere until the fields are ripe for harvest.

Take a stand-up break. Invite participants to help themselves to refreshments.

PART 2 (45/60 minutes)

Personal Testimonies (10/15 minutes)
1. Ask volunteers to share results of this week's family worship. As problems surface, direct members to the group for suggestions. Review points in "How to Conduct Family Worship" (member book, p. 97) as needed. Say, This is probably the only worship time that is more difficult to establish than a quiet time. If you are persistent, you will find the best time, place, and plan for your family. Continue even if all members of the family cannot or will not participate. God may use your faithfulness to convict other family members of their need to worship.

2. Ask group members to share their experiences in preparing a message from a Bible study. Ask one or two volunteers to present their outlines. Tell them they may have opportunities in the days ahead to give this message as part of their ordinary responsibilities.

MasterBuilder(10/15 minutes)
3. Ask members to work in pairs to present to each other the MasterBuilder presentation through the stage of the Disciple Maker. If both members did not have time to present it in last week's session, let the member who did not present go first this time.

"An Adventure in Ministry" (15 minutes)

4. Call attention to "An Adventure in Ministry" (member book, p. 115). Review the main points. Answer questions that are raised. Discuss the implications of all believers having the privilege and responsibility of being ministers. Say, This will help you begin the adventure of exploring basic Christian ministries. The material contains simple instructions on how to explore the ministries in which you are interested. What you want to do related to a ministry may be as simple or as complex as you desire. For example, you may want to make your first action that of having family worship. If so, plan a ministry action for your family this week.

Accountability Partners (5 minutes)

5. Call attention to the second activity on page 120 in the member book. Ask, How well are you discipling yourself? Suggest that members consider having accountability partners. Encourage them to think about the extent to which they want others to monitor their progress. Different personality types like different levels of accountability. One partner may want a regular, complete checkup in which the other partner takes the initiative; another may want to be checked only on certain things and not about anything the partners have not agreed on. The best arrangement is when both partners prefer the same level. Also suggest an additional alternative of having an accountability group that meets weekly to check on one another.

Next Week's Assignments (5/10 minutes)

6. Ask members to look at "My Walk with the Master This Week" for week 6. Review the specific assignments. Make sure members understand how to complete each assignment.

7. Remind members that they need to have all assignments in every "My Walk with the Master This Week" completed by the Spiritual-Gifts Workshop.

8. Briefly preview the content of week 6. Ask members to complete week 6, "Ministering as Colaborers," before Group Session 6.

9. Briefly review the traits of a colaborer in ministry (member book, pp. 107-8). Members will learn this part of MasterBuilder during week 6. Members should be prepared to present all of MasterBuilder in their own words by the end of week 6. If you see that some members are having difficulty mastering this presentation, offer to spend additional time with them after the session or loan them the videotape of this presentation to help them complete this assignment.

10. Review final details about the Spiritual-Gifts Workshop. Distribute maps if necessary. Invite questions. Provide information about trans-

portation to the site if the workshop is held away from your regular meeting area. Ask for volunteers to provide rides for others if needed.

11. Call attention to the week 6 assignment about taking the Spiritual-Gifts Inventory and scoring it. This needs to be completed before the Spiritual-Gifts Workshop. Members may need extra time; if so, they can finish the inventory between Group Session 6 and the workshop.

12. Close with prayer. Thank God for the progress members have made so far. Ask God to grant them courage, wisdom, and efficient use of time in the week ahead to prepare for the Spiritual-Gifts Workshop.

AFTER THE SESSION

❑ Send a written announcement giving information about the Spiritual-Gifts Workshop. Encourage each person to be present. See sample invitation below.

In acknowledgment of your walk with the Master
and to celebrate your completion of
MasterLife 4: The Disciple's Mission,
you are cordially invited to attend a
Spiritual-Gifts Workshop
(time • date • place)

Please bring your book indicating your completed assignments and
your completed and scored Spiritual-Gifts Inventory.

❑ If the Spiritual-Gifts Workshop is held away from the meeting site, furnish a phone number where members could be reached in an emergency. Furnish other instructions if members are to bring a sack lunch or snacks.
❑ Pray for members as they prepare for the Spiritual-Gifts Workshop.
❑ Call anyone who might be tempted not to attend the Spiritual-Gifts Workshop because of incomplete assignments. Help that person if he or she needs it.
❑ Take two members with you to minister or to witness. By now you should have taken everyone in the group with you at least once during this study.
❑ Contact the meeting site for the Spiritual-Gifts Workshop to confirm arrangements for food, space, and other matters as needed. Arrange for any materials you need for the workshop.
❑ Read "Before the Session" for week 6 to evaluate the amount of time you will need to prepare. At the top of the week 6 material record when you will prepare.

Split-Session Plan

FIRST WEEK
1. Follow the Standard Plan for the introduction and for checking each other's work in "My Walk with the Master This Week."

2. Lead week 5, "Training Disciples," reviewing items 3-12 only. Items 13-17 pertain to materials members will study next week.

3. Preview next week's assignments. Assign members days 4-5 in the study. During this preview, look only at the assignments they will be responsible for next week.

SECOND WEEK
Follow the Standard Plan for part 2. Spend about three minutes reviewing what members learned during the first week of this study. Ask volunteers to summarize important points from last week's study. Then move on to questions 13-17.

One-to-One Plan

Follow instructions for the Standard Plan. Encourage the person to be self-disciplined. Give help only if he or she fails to do an assignment. Be a servant. Challenge the person to a high standard of excellence.

GROUP SESSION 6

Ministering as Colaborers

Session Goals
By the end of this session, members will be able to demonstrate their progress toward *MasterLife* goals by ...
• completing week 6 assignments;
• preparing for the Spiritual-Gifts Workshop;
• presenting MasterBuilder in their own words;
• planning a special time to spend with the Lord in prayer;
• testifying of increased self-discipline and/or reporting a plan to work on self-discipline;
• telling how they plan to find their areas of ministry;
• recalling six ways to help them determine their spiritual gifts.

Standard Plan

BEFORE THE SESSION

❑ Review week 6 of *MasterLife 4: The Disciple's Mission* and read the activities for the Spiritual-Gifts Workshop.

❑ Pray daily for members of the *MasterLife* group. Some may become hesitant as they approach the Spiritual-Gifts Workshop. Ask God for guidance and encouragement in each member's life.

❑ Call members to confirm their attendance at the final group session and the Spiritual-Gifts Workshop.

❑ Master this week's material in the leader guide.

❑ Review the goals for this session.

❑ Check with the host and/or hostess to be sure he or she is prepared for the group this week.

❑ Arrange the meeting place so that members can sit in a circle.

❑ Finalize plans for the Spiritual-Gifts Workshop so you can share them with group members in this week's session. Have extra invitations on hand in case some members have not received theirs.

❑ Practice what you are suggesting members do to prepare for the workshop by making sure you complete and score your Spiritual-Gifts Inventory.

❑ Be sure you are up-to-date on all assignments before you ask members to have theirs completed.

❑ Have pens or pencils and extra blank paper on hand for the session.

❑ Plan your special time to spend with the Lord after the Spiritual-Gifts Workshop. Be prepared to report to the group how you will schedule this special time.

DURING THE SESSION

PART 1 (45/60 minutes)

Introduction (15/20 minutes)
1. Greet members. Ask members to share one change they have seen in the life of the person seated to their right since beginning *MasterLife 4: The Disciple's Mission*.

2. Ask volunteers to recall the mission of a disciple. (*A disciple's mission is to glorify God just as Jesus glorified Him; see John 17:1-4.*)

3. Ask, How do you plan to pass on what God has taught you during *MasterLife*? Are you open to lead or colead a *MasterLife* group?

4. Report on your plans for a special time to spend with the Lord after the Spiritual-Gifts Workshop. Invite members to share their plans.

5. Refer members to "How Shall They Hear?" (member book, p. 112-13). Invite a volunteer to read each point and tell what it means for him or her.

6. Pray together as a group that each of you will continue to grow and that each of you will continue to multiply disciples.

"My Walk with the Master" (10/15 minutes)

7. Pair members with persons other than their spouses to check each other's "My Walk with the Master This Week." Instruct members to use any extra time to review Scriptures memorized. Members are to have all assignments checked off by the end of the Spiritual-Gifts Workshop. If members still have assignments they have not completed, suggest they review these during the break. Offer to stay a few minutes after the session to work with members individually. Or consider scheduling a special time with them between the close of this session and the beginning of the Spiritual-Gifts Workshop.

"Ministering as Colaborers" (20/25 minutes)

Choose from the following activities those that are appropriate for your group's study. Do not exceed the time allowance.

8. Ask volunteers to define *spiritual gifts* in their own words. Discuss the difference between spiritual gifts and the fruit of the Spirit (see member book, p. 106). Ask members to distinguish between spiritual gifts and talents. (*Talents are received at the time of natural birth; spiritual gifts, at the time of spiritual birth.*)

9. Say, Respond to this statement: "Talents inspire or entertain; gifts are used to build up the church." After discussion, say, Spiritual gifts provide spiritual power and motivation. Talents that have been committed to God can be vehicles for God to use. Talents are often the vehicles through which spiritual gifts are expressed.

10. Ask, Who has spiritual gifts, and how many can a person have? (*Every Christian has at least one spiritual gift and often several. No one has all the gifts. The body of Christ will always be interdependent.*) Who decides which spiritual gift(s) a person has? (*Holy Spirit; see 1 Cor. 12:11*)

11. Say, Respond to the statement of a Christian leader, "As I look out over a congregation, I see row after row of unopened packages—gifts God has given to the church that have not been used." Ask, How does such a statement relate to the proper functioning of the body?

12. Ask members if they are faithfully serving God with their gifts. (*Some are, though they may not have identified which spiritual gifts they are using. Many are not, because they have not discovered their gifts.*) Ask

members what they think would happen if all God's people discovered their spiritual gifts and used them.

13. Ask, How can spiritual gifts be misused? (*gain a power base in a church, for self-glory, for spiritual pride, for personal profit, or teaching false doctrine.*) How can the abuse or misuse of spiritual gifts be avoided? (*By using them under the guidance of the Holy Spirit and the local congregation who follow biblical instruction; see 1 Cor. 12:26-30.*)

14. Lead the group to brainstorm ways they can bring unity in the body of Christ by using their spiritual gifts.

15. Ask members to list the six ways they can gain awareness of their gifts. Invite testimonies of how members learned more about their spiritual gifts by using this list.

16. Invite volunteers to tell the group gift(s) they have and why they think they have that gift(s).

17. Ask, How can we be ambassadors for Christ? What is our role in the Great Commission?

18. Close in prayer. Ask God to help members discover their spiritual gifts, particularly as the Spiritual-Gifts Workshop approaches.

Take a stand-up break. Invite participants to help themselves to refreshments

PART 2 (45-60 minutes)

Self-Discipline and Accountability (10/15 minutes)
1. Ask, How do you plan to continue to be disciplined after *MasterLife?* Are you growing in self-discipline? Ask volunteers to share their biggest challenges to being disciplined. Invite members to share who they have determined will be an accountability partner. Pray, asking God to help members hold firm to being disciplined.

MasterBuilder (15/20 minutes)
2. Ask members to pair with someone with whom they have not yet worked. Ask one member to give the MasterBuilder presentation through the Spiritual Disciple section. Instruct the other member to give the same portion of the presentation until you call time. If any member is still having difficulty with this presentation, offer to stay after the session to help. Or arrange a special one-to-one time with him or her between now and the Spiritual-Gifts Workshop.

"An Adventure in Ministry" (10 minutes)

3. Ask, How did you react to "An Adventure in Ministry"? Ask volunteers to identify what areas of ministry they explored this week. Ask, What did you learn about the ministry by doing a study of the ministry? How do you plan to learn more about the ministry? Has anyone already performed a ministry action connected with the ministry? Say, The Spiritual-Gifts Workshop will help you discover your spiritual gifts and will focus on one area of ministry for which you have been gifted.

Spiritual-Gifts Workshop (10/15 minutes)

4. Remind members that they are to have completed the Spiritual-Gifts Inventory by the workshop. Invite questions about the inventory or the scoring process. Ask members to read the definitions and characteristics of selected spiritual gifts (member book, p. 142) and be familiar with each one by the workshop.

5. Review what members should bring to the workshop: Bibles, completed inventory, completed assignments in *MasterLife 4: The Disciple's Mission.*

6. Distribute maps if the workshop is to be held away from the regular meeting place. Be sure transportation arrangements are made and members know of any food they are to bring. Provide a phone number where members can be reached during the workshop.

7. Assure members of your prayers for them as they make final preparation for the Spiritual-Gifts Workshop. Close with prayer. Thank God for the progress members have made. Ask God to give them courage, wisdom, and efficient use of time in the days before the workshop. Pray that God will prepare their hearts to learn more about their spiritual gifts and that they will discover their areas of ministry.

AFTER THE SESSION

❑ Meet with those who did not finish their assignments or could not explain MasterBuilder in their own words. Offer individual help as needed. Encourage these members to attend the workshop even if they do not complete all assignments beforehand.

❑ Pray for members as they prepare for the Spiritual-Gifts Workshop.

❑ Meet with members to discuss future discipleship opportunities. Affirm members with leadership potential and encourage them to become discipleship leaders in the church. Encourage all members to continue to grow in their discipleship by implementing *MasterLife* principles and practices in their lives and by participating in other discipleship studies.

❑ Contact the workshop meeting site to make final arrangements for food, space, and other matters as needed. Gather materials you need for the workshop.

❑ Read "Before the Session" for the Spiritual-Gifts Workshop to evaluate the amount of preparation. At the top of the material, record when you will prepare.

Split-Session Plan

FIRST WEEK

1. Follow the Standard Plan for the introduction and for checking "My Walk with the Master This Week."

2. Lead "Ministering as Colaborers." Review items 8-14 only. Items 15-18 pertain to materials members will study next week.

3. Assign members days 4-5 in the study. Preview only the assignments they will be responsible for next week.

SECOND WEEK

1. Follow the Standard Plan for part 2. Lead "Ministering as Colaborers." Spend three minutes reviewing what members have learned. Ask volunteers to summarize important point from last week's study. Then move on to questions 15-18. Spend time discussing questions members might have about the Spiritual-Gifts Workshop. The workshop is not designed for a split session.

One-to-One Plan

Follow instructions for the Standard Plan. Spend time helping the person finalize his or her presentation of MasterBuilder. Your partner needs to give the entire presentation. Discuss when and how knowing the concepts of the pathway of spiritual growth has helped you. You may want to give your presentation of MasterBuilder as an example.

Spiritual-Gifts Workshop

<table>
<tr><td>

Workshop Goals
By the end of this workshop, members will be able to demonstrate their progress toward *MasterLife* goals by …
- identifying their spiritual gift(s) and the ministry areas in which they are most gifted to serve;
- having their spiritual gift(s) confirmed and evaluated by others;
- confirming the gifts, goals, and talents of others for use in Christian ministry;
- hearing others suggest spiritual gifts they may not be aware of;
- planning next steps in discipling.

</td></tr>
</table>

BEFORE THE WORKSHOP

❑ Call group members and encourage them to attend. Remind them to complete the Spiritual-Gifts Inventory and score it before the workshop. Make sure all members understand that they are to bring to this meeting their completed workbooks.

❑ Master the Spiritual-Gifts Workshop material in the leader guide.

❑ Review the goals for the workshop.

❑ Check with the persons responsible for the workshop site to be sure they are ready for the group this week.

❑ Make plans for starting future *MasterLife* groups and for leader training so you can announce these plans to members who may want to lead groups. The optional training plan for multiple leaders (pp. 16-20 in this guide) provides training plans.

❑ Have pens or pencils and extra blank paper on hand for the workshop.

❑ Pray for members as they prepare for the workshop. Pray that members will have a sense of accomplishment at the end of this final time together in *MasterLife 4: The Disciple's Mission*.

❑ Enlist a group member or someone outside the group to facilitate the second of two groups you

will form for the spiritual-gifts activity. Before the workshop meet with the second facilitator and review what you expect of him or her.

❑ Prepare a card for each member. Write one of the following questions on the card.
- What is the funniest thing that has happened to you during *MasterLife*?
- What is the most embarrassing thing that has happened to you during *MasterLife*?
- What are you most proud of as a result of *MasterLife*?
- What are you most thankful for as a result of *MasterLife*?

❑ Ask members to decorate the meeting place for a celebration time (optional). Members may want to bring snacks to have at the conclusion of the workshop.

❑ Have on hand one *MasterLife* pin for each member. Prepare to present the pins to those who have completed all four studies of *MasterLife*. You may want to repeat this presentation in a church or group commissioning service.

❑ Check with church leaders to see if they would like to plan a commissioning service for members completing all four books of *MasterLife*. Be prepared to announce this to your members if plans have been made. If you have no plans for a churchwide commissioning service, plan to do this in your group at the conclusion of the workshop.

❑ Consider planning a group outreach activity to occur two or three weeks after *MasterLife*. Members should invite lost friends or relatives. Plan an event such as a coffee, barbecue, or outing. Ask someone to give a 10- to 15-minute personal testimony. Select a person who would attract lost people to his or her life story. At the conclusion of the testimony, dessert could be served while members circulate among the guests. They may ask, What did you think of that? Or, Does that make sense to you? This may lead to a witnessing opportunity.

DURING THE WORKSHOP

Announcements (5 minutes)

1. If you meet on Sunday afternoon and begin with lunch, encourage members to finish as soon as possible so that you may begin on time. Keep the meal simple. An elaborate meal takes more time, and some members will want to clean up instead of starting the Spiritual-Gifts Workshop.

2. If you are meeting in an unfamiliar site, inform members of the location of rest rooms, water fountains, and telephones.

3. If you plan to have the celebration, tell members that everyone is expected to stay until the completion of the Spiritual-Gifts Workshop before they begin to prepare for the celebration.

Instructions (10 minutes)

4. Ask members to turn to "Definitions of Spiritual Gifts" (member book, p. 142). Briefly review the definitions of each gift. Ask if members have questions about the definitions.

5. Read Ephesians 4:11-16 from the *Good News Bible*.

6. Explain that the purpose of this workshop is to help members: (1) declare and discuss their spiritual gifts, (2) confirm each other's gifts, and (3) identify gifts they may not be aware of.

Spiritual-Gifts Review (75/105 minutes)

7. Ask members to form two groups. You will facilitate one group, and the person you enlisted to help will facilitate the other group. Instruct them to mark on their spiritual-gifts diagrams (member book, p. 142) the gifts they think they have in each area. If they feel strongly, they should put their check mark in pencil close to the center of the wedge near the circle. If they feel reasonably sure but not totally certain they have a gift, they should place their mark in the middle of the pie-shaped section. If they think they might have a gift but strongly question it, they should mark near the edge of the wedge. Ask members to maintain silence and meditate on the definitions until everyone has made his or her marks.

8. Ask each person to share within his or her group by answering these questions:
- Why did you place your mark where you did?
- What has happened in your life that confirms the presence of this gift?
- At what level did you place your mark? Why?
- How deep is your conviction about this gift?

Ask members to let others see their diagrams as they explain them.

9. After each individual has declared his or her gifts, ask the other members to give feedback by affirming what the member has said about his or her gift. If members perceive a gift in the person that she or he has not declared, they can express that at this time. Or members may reply that they haven't seen this gift in the person and ask for more evidence that the member believes he or she has the gift. Ask the individual these questions:
- Do your gifts cluster in one area of ministry?
- Which gifts do you need to balance your gifts? For example, if a person has the gift of prophecy, this person usually needs someone working with him or her who has the practical gift of helps; someone with the gift of mercy needs someone alongside him or her who has gift of spiritual discernment. These gifts appear directly across from each other on the diagram. The purpose of this activity is to help members recognize their need for each other in the body of Christ.
- In what areas of service do you believe you can use these gifts? Ask the person to think about the ministries depicted on the Disciple's Cross as he or she considers a ministry.

Ask members to continue to give feedback as this person shares. Repeat the process for each member.

10. After each person has shared and others have given feedback, call the group to a time of conversational prayer. Group members should gather around each person and pray for that person's use of his or her spiritual gifts. Then move on to the next person in the group. Members can spend as long as 15 to 20 minutes with each person in prayer.

11. Lead the following discussion within each small group. Turn to each person and ask, If our *MasterLife*

group represented a church, where would the emphasis of our church be? Would it be balanced, or would it lean toward the ministry of service, or teaching, or worshiping? Are we strong in some areas and weak in others? Do we need other kinds of gifts on our team?

12. Reassemble the total group and allow members to briefly express their reaction to this spiritual-gifts review. Recognize that for some members this may be the first time to participate in a discussion of spiritual gifts.

Celebrate (20/25 minutes)

This time is designed to help members express their feelings about the course and about each other. Make it a fun time.

13. Give each member one of the cards you prepared. Have each person ask four different members the question written on his or her card and record their answers. Members will continue this activity until each person has collected an answer from at least four different members. Of course, everyone will also have given an answer to several different questions. When all have finished asking questions and giving answers, ask them to be seated.

14. Invite a volunteer to tell one of the answers he or she was given without identifying the person. Ask members to guess who said it. The first person to guess tells one of his or her answers. Members are invited to guess who made that statement, and so on. This activity continues until time runs out. Limit this to 15 minutes. If no one identifies the person who made a certain statement, the person who made the statement will identify himself or herself. That person will then take his or her turn reporting an answer received from another person.

Presentation of *MasterLife* Pins (10/15 minutes)

15. Announce that you will give pins to those who have completed the requirements for the four *MasterLife* studies.

16. Present the pins. Give a word of encouragement as you place the pin on each person's lapel.

Conclusion (5 minutes)

17. If some members want to stay and talk or pray, encourage them to do so. Do not go overtime unless all members agree to do so. Members may have other plans; need to relieve a baby-sitter; or if the workshop is on Sunday, need to get home and make preparations to return to church.

18. Sound a note of victory and excitement about the completion of *MasterLife 4: The Disciple's Mission*. For many members this may conclude 24 weeks of study in *MasterLife*.

19. Some members may express interest in leading a *MasterLife* group. Announce the time, date, and place of the next leader training and the beginning of the next *MasterLife* groups.

20. Announce any plans for involving the church in a commissioning service. Such a service provides a way to tell the church that group members have dedicated themselves to becoming servants. Members may be invited to share their testimonies about what Christ has done for them during this training period. Caution members not to sound proud or exclusive.

21. Close with a prayer of thanksgiving and celebration.

AFTER THE WORKSHOP

❑ Make sure the building or meeting facility is in order before you leave. Be a servant.
❑ Write to members expressing appreciation for their participation in the study. Remind them that you are praying as they continue to apply concepts of *MasterLife 4: The Disciple's Mission* to daily life and about how they will use the spiritual gift(s) God has given them.
❑ Evaluate the entire *MasterLife* experience. List the things you think were most helpful. Make another list of things to avoid in future groups.
❑ Evaluate your leadership during *MasterLife 4: The Disciple's Mission*. This will help you as you plan to lead future groups. Go back to some of the questions this leader guide suggested you ask yourself.
❑ Spend time in prayer for each member.

❑ Make plans for future *MasterLife* groups and other training that will be needed after *MasterLife*. Begin to talk to members who show an interest in leading a future *MasterLife* group. For more information about other discipleship courses, request a catalog from Adult Ministry Publishing; One LifeWay Plaza; Nashville, TN 37234-0175.

❑ Inform the church through publications and announcements the outcome of the group and of the *MasterLife* experience in general, since many of these members have been in *MasterLife* for 24 weeks and many life changes likely will have occurred. Inform the appropriate church-staff members about potential leaders who emerged during the course, especially as a result of the Spiritual-Gifts Workshop. You may ask members to share brief testimonies about what *MasterLife* has meant to them or their salvation testimonies. Announce that the church is accepting the names of persons who want to enroll in *MasterLife*.

Split-Session Plan

The Spiritual-Gifts Workshop is not designed for split sessions.

One-to-One Plan

1. The Spiritual-Gifts Workshop lends itself to a one-to-one approach. Help the person evaluate his or her inventory. Follow the instructions for the Standard Plan about how to help the person assess what he or she has discovered. Follow this procedure for the person you are discipling first; then let him or her follow the same procedure with you.

2. Instead of the group procedures given for the celebration, plan a special occasion such as going out to eat together. Talk over the things that have been the funniest, have been the most embarrassing, or have made you thankful and proud. Share your visions together and pray for each other.

3. If the person has completed all four studies, give him or her the *MasterLife* pin individually or at a scheduled group meeting with his or her peers. Plan for future discipleship training that relates to this person's needs. Encourage the person to receive the best training available from other equippers. Read 1 Corinthians 4:15-16. You are responsible for helping the person reach his or her full potential as a colaborer.

Learn the Secrets of Intimacy with God

You were created for fellowship with God. Through prayer you communicate with the Father and deepen your relationship with Him.

This classic, in-depth study will lead you to develop intimacy with God and effectiveness in your prayer life. As you examine biblical examples and apply biblical prayer principles, your relationship with God will grow fresher every day.

Disciple's Prayer Life will teach you how to—
- develop a richer prayer life;
- discover the unique way God relates to you;
- give thanks and worship God;
- use Scripture in prayer and make decisions based on biblical principles;
- pray with others;
- confess sin;
- apply principles of asking;
- deal with unanswered prayer and hindrances to prayer;
- pray for yourself, others, and missions;
- develop a prayer ministry;
- continue growing in fellowship with God.

No matter where you are in your walk with God, you can develop a deeper, more intimate relationship with Him. *Disciple's Prayer Life* will show you the way. (ISBN 0-7673-3494-9)

To order this resource: WRITE LifeWay Church Resources Customer Service, One LifeWay Plaza, Nashville, TN 37234-0113; FAX order to (615) 251-5933; PHONE 1-800-458-2772; EMAIL *CustomerService@lifeway.com*; order ONLINE at *www.lifeway.com*; or visit the LifeWay Christian Store serving you.